Michael Sheane

ARTHUR H. STOCKWELL LTD.
Torrs Park   Ilfracombe   Devon

British Library Cataloguing-in-Publication Data.
A catalogue record for this book is available
from the British Library.

Dedication:
To the memory of my mother

By the same author:
Ulster & Its Future After the Troubles (1977)
Ulster & The German Solution (1978)
Ulster & The British Connection (1979)
Ulster & The Lords of the North (1980)
Ulster & The Middle Ages (1982)
Ulster & Saint Patrick (1984)
The Twilight Pagans (1990)
Enemy of England (1991)

ISBN 0 7223 3448-6
Printed in Great Britain by
Arthur H. Stockwell Ltd.
Torrs Park   Ilfracombe
Devon

Contents

Chapter 1

The Planters

There were planters or colonizers in the region of Derry long before the London Companies set up their plantation around Saint Columba's old monastery. The problem from the beginning was that there were a large number of native Irish Catholics, who resented the Protestant presence. Derry had seen invasions many hundreds of years before, with the arrival of the Vikings about AD795. In 1600, when Docwra came with a few hundred men, the clans were determined that they would make life difficult for the English. In 1600, Elizabeth I was on the British throne, but she was coming to the end of her days. When some of the native Irish aristocracy, who had rebelled against English rule, took ship for Europe in 1607, it meant that the English could build an Irish colony. They were not discouraged by the fate of the Munster plantation in south-west Ireland, where a substantial number of British had perished.

With the defeat of Hugh O'Neill in 1603, the British were confident that the planting of Derry would be simple and that similar plantations throughout Ireland would bear fruit. The ideal was that the number of planters at Derry should match the number of Irish. Sir Henry Docwra's plantation of 1600 was a response to the O'Neill wars. It so happened that the building of a fortresses at Derry in 1600 acted as a northern front against O'Neill. Derry thereafter was considered a fit place to make the main British plantation in Ulster.

A period of about eighty-nine years elapsed between the coming of English ships to Lough Foyle to the siege of Derry in 1689. In between this time, came the bloody 1641 rebellion of the Irish Catholics against the colonizers, but rebellion did not discourage the British in Ulster.

Those English who came to Derry or Derry-Calgach — "the Oak Grove of the Fierce Warrior" — were not put off by the bad climate in the region — a rainy and damp climate that the English hated. The colonizers in 1600 were soldiers, and their character was determined by the loose morality of the age. The Irish were equally immoral and violent, and from the beginning, as the foundations were laid, to the conflict of 1689, both sides put forward their unruly elements to fight for what they believed was right. The Protestants, at first mostly Anglicans, saw nothing immoral about ejecting the Catholics from the richer lands around the hill of the new town. The Catholics, for their part, hit back with atrocities in an effort to regain their lands.

5

A planter had to be strong and hardy in order to contain the Roman Catholics. These planters were always homesick and from the beginning they undertook their duties half-heartedly. The planter hit back when the Irish attacked; apart from driving the Catholics off their lands, they did not go out of their way to unnecessarily persecute "the Papists". The lands around Derry would yield rich revenue for the Crown, and all the various trades had their allotments, when the London Companies started to seriously "plant" the region. The ideal was that the Protestants should have as many children as possible, so that the number of British would exceed the number of Catholics, who bred profusely as well. The planter could offer his offspring a good life around Derry. The second and third generations would regard the newly-won lands as theirs as a matter of course, and they would become Protestant Irishmen, with a strong attachment and loyalty to the British Crown.

The Protestants at Derry paid only lip service to Anglicanism, whilst the Irish Catholics were more devout in their faith. The colonizers from Britain had heard about the rich lands in Ulster and elsewhere in Ireland, and from the beginning the motivation for plantation in Ulster, particularly in the region of Derry, was economic. Out of this situation, as Protestantism developed, arose the devout planter, who steadfastly held out at Londonderry from December 1688 to July 1689. The second and third generations of planters, whilst becoming more religious, were on the other hand becoming very anti-Roman Catholic, a situation that obtained in the England of James II, under whom the siege of the city began. The mainland British were more moral perhaps than the Protestants sent to Derry. The Anglicans of Derry, worshipping in Saint Columb's Cathedral, and in their little wooden and stone churches in the countryside around the city, were not on a religious crusade. Most of their energies were devoted to developing the land and making dishonest returns on revenue gained to London. Catholics were thankful that at least Protestants at Derry did not make any effort to evangelize a religion that the state outlawed. If a Catholic king however came to the throne, the situation might be different — with the Londonderry planters persecuted and King James I wanting to return the hard won Protestant lands to Roman Catholics.

The picture of the early planter at Derry is one of a hard drinking and overeating Protestant — a generation that found themselves Protestant because of the wiles of Henry VIII and the determination of Elizabeth I. The planter was living in fear, perhaps in greater fear than the Catholics. The Catholics committed great atrocities against the planters in the rebellion of 1641, a rebellion which the Protestants always had in mind when James II came to the throne in England, and which motivated them to hold out so long against this Catholic monarch. The planter feared mutilation as well as losing his land, so these early colonizers were armed to the teeth, albeit with inefficient weapons; but the walls around their city were such that they might incite the disciples of Vauban to laughter. But Ulster was a virgin land, like the lands in the United States, with the difference that the Red Indians were small in numbers, and where the White

Man ruled over the Redskin with efficient weapons. It is doubtful if these early Anglicans read their Bible in the original plantation of 1609, and it is equally doubtful that the populace of Londonderry, probably largely illiterate in 1689, had any idea about the morals of rebellion against a Catholic monarch. In 1609–10 the people of Derry would always eagerly await news from the home country, as ships pulled into the little harbour of the River Foyle on their voyage from Chester. To be sure they were anxious to know if the Britain of James I was still Protestant. Political parties in England had just been conceived by the times of Charles II, and in 1685 — when the Catholic James II came to the throne, the ships coming from Chester brought bad news. It was as well that the Protestants at Londonderry had built those walls in 1613, even though they were somewhat neglected. The news from the countryside was almost always alarming. Travellers calling in at Londonderry, galloping over the rough tracks, told a story of Catholic sullenness. The ships brought news about the position of England's own kith and kin back to the House of Commons, which was determined to look after the Protestants of the city. The planters had no ideas about separation from England, for Westminster wanted to aid the planters' efforts in Ireland. Londonderry was a colony, for the English had been in Ireland since 1169, when the kings of England were lords of the country.

The object of the 1600 plantation was to eventually make Ulster as English as England itself. The political term to describe the British state was the United Kingdom of Great Britain and Ireland. The planters were aware, as the 'colony' developed, that Ireland — and Derry as a city — was not treated as an equal with other mainland institutions. There was perhaps always that element of doubt in the planters' mind whether England would honour its obligations in Ulster. Fear of the Catholics and distrust of the English, for the second and third generations, was a theme that ran through the Ulster situation. The problem was that the sea divided Ireland from England. A further problem lay in the English attitude to the Irish, who were treated as second-class citizens. If the situation got out of hand at Londonderry, Britain might lose interest in her Irish realm and leave the planters alone to manage the Irish. Londonderry's leaders assured the citizens of the city that England always had the interests of her north-west plantation at heart and that there were no traitors amongst the leadership.

As the 1609 plantation developed, many of the 10,000 Anglicans and 80,000 Lowland Scots in the Province, lost interest in the scheme and returned home. Perhaps at this early stage, the planters saw the task of making the Irish British — or subjecting them to English rule — as impossible. The city of Londonderry was more like a fortress than a city, with its stone walls erected to keep the Catholics out. From an early date there was no attempt to reconcile the two races — or indeed to leave the Irish alone, despite the fact that many Protestants returned home, and in the beginning did not undertake their duties with enthusiasm; i.e., there was an initial reluctance to remove Catholics from the lands around the city. The Irish did not organize themselves into a united body

7

to eject the Protestants, despite the O'Dogherty rebellion in 1608, when a native Irish chieftain rose up, and stormed out of Donegal to devastate Derry. This was the kind of event the Anglicans — and later the Scots — feared; a sudden Catholic attack and indiscriminate slaughter of men, women and children. The planters were encouraged by the fact that the Irish had never shown much unity in the face of England. For the men of Londonderry, there was a future for planter civilization, and there was confidence that despite the superior Catholic numbers, the plantation in the north-west would last. The English had been persistent in Ireland up to a point, although the tendency had always been to cultivate fortresses in 'civilized' areas such as the Pale and to leave the interior and the north of the country to the Irish.

The planters at Londonderry understood the Catholics well. Politics and religion were one issue in those days, but for Catholics, kept out of the city, their religion was everything. As the Protestants took their lands, chasing them out of their homes, they did not lose faith. Equally the Protestants, always under threat from the Catholics, did not forsake Anglicanism or Presbyterianism. Even though Britain sometimes hesitated over her Irish colony, the Protestants of County Londonderry and the rest of Ulster, did not forsake their attachment to the British monarchy. In 1600 the first serious attempt was made to make Ireland, and Ulster, British by the settlers that England sent out. The task was easier now that the native Irish aristocracy had been defeated in 1603. In 1603 Ireland, particularly Ulster, was demoralized, and the planters at Londonderry had a chance to make the lands they were given by the Crown, Protestant lands for the second and third generations. The problem was that the Catholics had long memories and would not forget that they once held the richer lands. By 1688 the hatred of Protestant against Catholic was as bad as ever.

The planter was a human being like everyone else. There were those amongst them that had sympathy for Catholics, and amongst Catholics, those who had sympathy for Protestants. The planter had a wife and children and had responsibilities. This meant maintaining his position and keeping the main plantation in Ulster at Londonderry, Protestant. The planter feared for his family and what the Catholics might do to them, and likewise the Catholics did not like what the Protestants were doing to their families, by denying them their lands. For the planter, land and money were a measure of wealth, whilst the Gael looked upon cattle as the main measure of a man; but cattle were no good to him if he had not the right lands on which to pasture his animals.

In Ulster, the planter took everything, for the six counties of Coleraine, Armagh, Tyrone, Donegal, Cavan and Monaghan were escheated to the Crown. The new Lord-Deputy, Sir Arthur Chichester, was like most of his contemporaries, a Catholic hater, and warned the Protestants that the 'Romanists' might rise up against the plantation, a prediction that came true in 1641. The situation at Londonderry was of the Protestants' own making, but as human beings the planters only reflected the temper of the age.

Londonderry therefore was an outpost of British civilization; outside of the planter territories lay the Irish, who knew nothing about cultivated arts and who deserved to be suppressed because they had failed to achieve unity under their ancient High-Kings. At Londonderry the average Protestant boy or girl was educated to believe that British rule was right and that Roman Catholicism was a heresy. The planter believed that the Pope was in league with the Devil, and the abject condition of the Irish confirmed this view. The planter was a human being, so he gave in to the opinions of the darker side of his nature, but Catholics were human beings as well, just like in the Modern Age Communists and Capitalists give in to the bleaker aspects of their ideology.

From the beginning, the plantation at Londonderry did not go right, a period that started in 1600 until the siege of the city in 1689. It was the Irish under command of a British king that laid siege to the Maiden City, a Catholic king, chased from his throne by a foreign and Protestant monarch, William III, a Calvinist. For nearly one hundred years Londonderry was politically under siege, for the Catholics longed for the date when they could take possession of the city and set up their own regime.

Chapter 2

The Eve of the Siege

On the eve of the siege of Londonderry in 1689, the population of the city was about 3,000; some of these made up of Catholics. The city, set upon a hill, and overlooked by high ground, measured about half a mile in length and was three-quarters of a mile broad. It stood on the right bank of the River Foyle. Lough Foyle and the Atlantic Ocean lay to the north of the Londonderry plantation, whilst County Donegal lay to the west; to the south-east of the city lay the Sperrin Mountains of the former County of Coleraine.

The city was situated on a bend in the river, and sailing down the Foyle in his curragh, a Gaelic boatman saw that the main feature of Londonderry were its walls. Sailing north he would pass the Shipquay, and he would observe Shipquay Gate, after he had passed Ferryquay Gate, overlooking the bend in the river. All the main streets of the city led to the Market House, whilst the cathedral and Bishop's Gate stood to the west of the Market House, also observed by our Gaelic boatman. The city would be difficult to lay siege to from the east, for the enemy would have to cross the River Foyle. An attack out of Donegal seemed the best line of approach. The O'Dohertys, O'Donnells, O'Cahans and O'Neills were still prowling around, and the walls were built not to withstand an attack by a professional army, but to withstand the onslaught of the dispossessed.

The Irish at first were inspired by the accession of the Catholic Duke of York to the throne, for now the city of Londonderry might be governed by a Catholic Mayor, and the Catholics given a greater share in the government of their country. Our Gaelic boatman, leaving his curragh on the mud banks of the River Foyle, might travel inland, aware that he was entering the plantation. He saw his land and his city occupied by many types of traders. To mention only some, there were the Mercers, Innholders, Cooks, Embroiderers, Masons, Grocers, Dryers, Tallow Chandlers, Fishmongers, Leather Sellers, Plasterers, Glaziers, Basket Makers, Musicians, Goldsmiths, Cordwinders, Painters, Armourers, Skinners, Stationers, White Bakers, Girdlers, Merchant Taylors, Turners, Founders, Salters, Dyers, Saddlers, Cutlers, Joiners, Woolmen, Haberdashers, Wax Chandlers, Ironmongers, Brewers, Scriveners, Coopers, Pewterers, Barber Surgeons, Carpenters, Vintners, Woodmongers, Weavers, Plumbers, Poulterers, Tilers and Bricklayers, Blacksmiths, Fruiterers, Curriers, Clothmakers, Overplus of Merchant Taylors, Butchers, Brown Bakers,

Upholsterers, Bowyers and Fletchers. Each of these trades had their lands and little houses and castle, so the plantation looked like a collection of small villages, which looked to Londonderry and the British connection to protect them against a Catholic uprising. There were more Protestants occupying the land as were occupying the city, so the entire Londonderry plantation numbered in the region of 100,000.

Life for the planter started at sun up, and they were glad when the long summer evenings came, for the planter always wondered who was knocking at his door, especially on a dark winter's night; then they would be huddled over their turf fires, talking about the truth of Protestantism and telling tales of the home country. The original planters of Docwra's day had to be content with houses made of rods and wattle and a lifestyle close to the Irish. Now, in 1685, the year of the Catholic James's accession, they occupied one-roomed cottages. On the eve of the siege, the Protestants did not think they had a future, and our Catholic boatman could boast that the corporation of Londonderry was mainly Catholic, although the Mayor, Cormac O'Neill, was a Protestant (his wife was a Catholic). The Lord-Deputy of Ireland, the Earl of Tyrconnel was an Irish Roman Catholic, and fanatical about his faith. Our Catholic boatman thought that the planters had not a future neither at Londonderry or anywhere else in Ireland, but this was not the case. There was no mass exodus of Protestants from the plantation with the accession of James II, for they resigned themselves to being governed by Roman Catholics. The hope of getting rid of the Catholics was always there, and if James put a foot wrong — as he did — then it was possible that Protestant rule would be restored. The planters of 1685-1688 considered themselves perhaps as Irish as the Irish themselves. They were a different sort of Irish men — Irish men that had acquired a 'national' identity at Londonderry.

These third generation planters could not suddenly leave the country for the safety of England and Scotland. The future for Londonderry Protestants lay in Ulster; they were Ulstermen and only extreme circumstances would make them leave their lands and city. The Mayor of Londonderry was a puppet of the Catholic Lord-Deputy Tyrconnel, and the planters were resolved that they should live side by side with Roman Catholics. As long as the planters held Catholic lands, reaping profits and sustenance, they were content to let James II have his way. For the majority of Protestants, so our Gaelic boatman observed, there was no question of rising up against the Roman Catholic corporation, a confrontation they would inevitably lose.

The Protestants knew that although he was a Roman Catholic, James II was also British, and they were certain that he would maintain the British position in Ireland. James had no particular liking for the Irish, and looked down upon them. It would appear that the Protestants feared the loss of their religion, whilst economic issues took second place. In 1688, on 7th December, when the thirteen Apprentice Boys closed the gates in front of a Catholic army, there was a strong case for not shutting them. James II had been chased from his throne because

11

he was a Roman Catholic, and his place had been taken by William of Orange. James fled to the France of Louis XIV, who half-heartedly backed him. France was the most powerful country in Europe, so the planters from the beginning seemed to be backing the wrong horse. From the start it was religion that the two races, Irish and British, were fighting over. If only the planters of Ireland would turn Roman Catholic, then there would not be a problem.

On the eve of the siege, siege was the last thing that Protestants wanted. The prosperity of the plantation depended upon peaceful conditions prevailing, so it was important to avoid another 1641. Our Catholic boatman also knew that Roman Catholics would put little faith in James to recover their lost lands. The only hope for them was that under a Catholic king, they could freely practise their religion and continue to control the corporation of the city. The Protestant future lay in maintaining friendly relations with Roman Catholics, and this the two Protestant factions, Anglicans and Presbyterians, worked for at all times. In the inns of the city and in the shops, Roman Catholics came and went, but it was the planter that could afford the civilized luxuries of the plantation and it was the Irishman that could only afford a modest supply of beer, despite the presence of a Catholic corporation.

It is hard to see how the Irish could radically alter their position at Londonderry, for the Protestants had been there since 1600. The fanatical Irishman, most likely a dispossessed aristocratic clansman, was perhaps for driving the Protestants back to England and Scotland; a task easily obtainable because of their small numbers.

Hatred of Protestant against Catholic — a religious situation — appears to have caused the events of 7th December 1688; in the same way religious differences caused the Glorious Revolution in England. The Protestants of the Londonderry plantation put their Protestantism before their lands. To submit to a Catholic king meant damnation, whereas to submit to a Protestant monarch meant similar damnation for Catholics. It is best understood by the modern notion of the average man in the Western world, who would die for democracy. Democracy today is more important than having a job, being a prosperous consumer, or going to church or chapel. It is a notion that is hard to explain, if it can be explained at all.

The Protestants of Londonderry and the rest of Ulster, by 1688, were prepared to lay down their lives for religious freedom; i.e., for the various forms of Protestantism. Anglicanism and Presbyterianism did not see eye to eye, but when confronted by the enemy, they were prepared to co-operate, just as Conservative and Labour parties co-operated during the Second World War. In 1688, Protestant fanaticism was at another peak, and had learnt nothing from the English Civil War and the excesses of Cromwell. Throughout Europe, Roman Catholicism was the party that ruled most states, and as we have seen, the France of Louis XIV, James's brother-in-law, was Roman Catholic.

It is not known how many Protestants fled the Kingdom when they knew trouble was looming, so presumably not all of them were fanatically Protestant or were over anxious about holding on to their lands. Perhaps they preferred to live in the England and Scotland of William of Orange rather than under the Catholicism of James II. More likely that there were timid elements within Protestantism, just as there were timid men in Roman Catholicism when Hugh O'Neill, Earl of Tyrone, fled to Europe in 1607, leaving his clanmen to the mercy of the planters.

On the eve of the siege, there were in the region of 100,000 Protestants in Ulster. Many of them fled via Londonderry, sailing down the Foyle, waiting for peaceful conditions to return. They left behind an Ireland which had a population of about 800,000 Catholics and a Catholic militia that was entirely under command of James's appointee for the Lord-Deputyship, the Earl of Tyrconnel who before being raised to the peerage, was known as Colonel Richard Talbot.

Tyrconnel reckoned that "the Catholiques of Ulster are not soe considerable by reason of the greater number of Scotch Presbyterians there". The Protestants would not give up in the North without a fight, and they had a local aristocracy to lead them. In County Down there was the Earl Mount-Alexander; in Antrim, Viscount Masserene, and Sir Arthur Rawdon, who was nicknamed 'Cock of the North' because of his fighting spirit. At a lower level there was Ezekiel Hopkins, the Anglican Bishop of Derry who preached submission to royal authority at all times and who believed in the Divine Right of Kings. On a still lower level there was the Reverend George Walker of Donoughmore in County Tyrone, who later reached the besieged city. It was he who was at first sympathetic with the Governor of the city, Robert Lundy, who was condemned by the citizens as a traitor, when he tried to surrender the town to James.

Tyrconnel had detachments of troops in the North, so our Gaelic boatman knew, stationed at Carrickfergus and the foot of Charlemont, five miles from Dungannon, in George Walker's country. At Derry there was a regiment that had escaped Tyrconnel's purge as he replaced the Protestant militias with Roman Catholic men. Lundy, a Lieutenant Colonel, was in this regiment, led by Lord Mountjoy, no relation of Elizabeth's great Lord-Deputy of ninety years earlier. 1641 would not come again as long as Mountjoy's regiments remained in the city. Matters stood tenderly balanced in 1688 with the corporation of the city having few men of British parents, and crammed with Catholics, and a Protestant militia intent upon preserving Londonderry's Protestant heritage. Tyrconnel was convinced that the Protestant militia at Londonderry had to the replaced, for Derry was a key fort in the north-west and the main port to Scotland from which an overthrown monarch such as James might make his way back to England to recover the Crown from William of Orange.

Our Gaelic boatman has been travelling around the plantation all day in the wintry weather of November 1688. Darkness fell about half-past four, so our Gael made his way back to his curragh, finding that the tide had now come in on the River Foyle. He decided that he wanted to visit Londonderry, so sailing down the Foyle, he drew his curragh up at the Shipquay. In the inns of the town he found that two men were mostly on the lips of Protestants — James II and Tyrconnel. Our Gael was certain that James would recover his kingdom and that the Earl of Tyrconnel, James's new Lord-Deputy, would look after Roman Catholics. There was talk of what might happen if Tyrconnel tried to replace the Protestant militia, but at this stage there was no talk of holding out in a siege of the city. At Saint Columb's Cathedral — our Gaelic boatman dare not enter it — Ezekiel Hopkins, the Bishop of Derry, was perhaps praying for peace. The Anglicans perhaps wanted to come to some sort of arrangement with James and Tyrconnel, whilst the Scots Presbyterians or Puritans held out fanatically for their faith, but they too prayed for peace.

The Catholic boatman stayed the night in the city, sure that with the coming of James to Ireland, Londonderry would fall entirely into Catholic hands. Tyrconnel had ordered that the Earl of Antrim should ride on Londonderry to replace the Protestant militia, and the date appointed for his arrival at the city was 20th November 1688. A confrontation between Protestants and Catholics was at hand, and the question now arose whether to let the aged Earl of Antrim, a Roman Catholic, within the city or to keep him out. As in modern Ulster, the Protestants were alarmed, and the cry of "No Surrender" was soon to be heard from Derry's walls.

Chapter 3

Roman Catholicism

Protestants in Londonderry could not accept that the Church of Rome represented the original faith of Christ. James II had been converted to the faith when he was Duke of York, and in 1685, when he ascended the throne, Protestants saw their beliefs threatened by a king who put the Pope in first place above all other monarchs. All Christians believed that the Bible was the basis of Christianity, but men like Tyrconnel and Alexander MacDonnell, third Earl of Antrim, argued about the composition of the Bible itself. The Roman Catholic version of the Bible consisted not only of the Old and New Testaments, but of the Apocrypha, which came between these two books. At the Reformation, the Protestants rejected the Apocrypha, along with all the other Catholic doctrines. The Catholic Church not only regarded the Bible as the basis of Christianity, but also looked to the writings of the Latin and Greek Church fathers, as inspiring a lot of Roman Catholic doctrines, and as infallible as Scripture.

Alexander MacDonnell, aged seventy-six, was convinced that the Bishop of Rome was head of the earthly Church and the final authority in interpreting Scripture. Ezekiel Hopkins however replaced an 'infallible' Pope with an infallible Bible. For Alexander, Roman Catholicism was a warm and colourful faith, whilst Protestantism was lifeless. Alexander nor the Lord-Deputy Tyrconnel could not understand why Protestants denied that the Church was an evolving body and that the Early Church looked to Rome as a fountainhead. Roman Catholics claimed that Christ had given a clear commission to Saint Peter, telling him that he was the Rock upon which the Church should be built. Peter subsequently went to Rome and became the first Pope to have the Church's headquarters in the city. At the Reformation, the Reformers did not deny that it was useful for the Church to have its headquarters in the Eternal City. What men like Luther objected to were the many doctrines and dogmas the Church of Rome claimed that were necessary to be held in order to obtain salvation. Men like Tyrconnel and Alexander MacDonnell regarded the Pope as the supreme ruler in Christendom. As far as men like Hopkins and Walker were concerned, the Church of Rome was in grievous error, for she taught doctrines and dogmas that were not biblical, for example the adoration of the Blessed Virgin Mary and transubstantiation. The Puritans regarded the Church of Rome as a tyrannical organization, for one man was deciding the faith of millions.

Roman Catholicism did not deny that it was likely that Saint Peter and the very early Popes did not indulge in Mariology, for as yet the Church had not developed the sophistication of thought of later centuries. The planters of Londonderry claimed that the Bible was Christ's final message to the Church, and that the Popes had no right to promulgate doctrines and dogmas that were not in it. The Church of Rome was ruled by bishops, and this Ezekiel Hopkins, the Anglican, did not disagree with, but for him the reigning monarch was head of the Church, a faith based upon the Bible. Roman Catholics cried out that the Puritans denied the Episcopalian Church; they denied the Pope, the archbishops, the bishops, the saints, and only had a very small role for Mary in their version of Christianity. It is doubtful if the average Roman Catholic Gael could understand the more colourful aspects of Catholicism, for illiteracy was rife. The average planter had a more simple faith to remember and practise, but they cried out that as well as having an important role for Christ in the faith, Roman Catholics 'worshipped' the Virgin Mary and used saints to intercede for them when they were praying.

Roman Catholics believed that their Church was the greatest single influence in history, for they could boast that there had been Popes at Rome for 1,688 years. The conditions the Irish lived under — the peasant in his daub and wattle hut — did not change their minds about their faith or made them love the Pope and the Virgin Mary less. For them there was nothing pagan about Roman Christianity and there was something Satanic about all forms of Protestantism. The Irish did not blame their Church for the political state of Gaeldom. The Gael did not think that his bishop or priest had a closed mind; on the contrary it was the Protestant bigots of the plantation that were narrow-minded.

Many priests in the Derry area were telling their congregations that a Divine Plan was at hand, which was too secret to tell the laity. The churls must play their part when the time came, but as we have seen, there were some priests who had sympathy for the plight of Protestants. During the first week of December, while Alexander MacDonnell was making his way to Londonderry, there occurred the strange incident of 'the Comber letter', which was found in the street in the little village of Comber in County Down. It was dated 3rd December 1688, and addressed to the Earl Mount-Alexander, and was marked 'To my Lord, this deliver with haste and care'. The writer of the letter promised to reveal his identity when it was safe, but this never happened. 'The Comber letter' appears to have been a hoax; it warned of another 1641. The letter read:—

Good my Lord, I have written to you to let you know that all our Irishmen through Ireland is sworn that on the ninth day of this month (December) *they are to fall on to kill and murder man, wife and child; and I desire your Lordship to take care of yourself and all others that are judged by our men to be heads, for whosoever can kill any of you, they are to have a captain's place, so my desire to your honour is to look to yourself and give other noblemen warning, and go not out either night or day without a good guard with you, and let no Irishman come near you, whatsoever he be; so this is all from him who was*

16

your father's friend, and is your friend and will be, though I dare not be known as yet for fear of my life.

When 9th December came around, despite alarm being raised all over Ulster, nothing happened. It seems strange that such a serious warning should have been dropped in the street, unless it was meant for eyes rather than the Earl Mount-Alexander. To be sure the people of Londonderry thought that the priests and friars were behind such a threat of rebellion. Despite assurances from Lord-Deputy Tyrconnel that the letter was a lie, the Protestants took the threat seriously; this at a time when the Earl of Antrim's regiment was about to enter the city. The letter and Lord Antrim's presence, proved to Protestants that all Roman Catholics were liars, the chief of which was Dick Talbot himself. If the city fell to Roman Catholicism, the Devil would reign, and the Popish priests would take over Saint Columb's Cathedral from the Anglicans, where the blasphemy of the Mass would be held.

'The Comber letter' provided fanatics at Londonderry with fresh evidence that rebellion was at hand and that all Catholics should be driven out of the city and the Romish corporation overthrown. The cathedral would reek with incense and statues of the Virgin and Child would disfigure Ezekiel Hopkins' place of worship. The Puritans were the fanatics, whilst the Anglicans took a more intellectual approach in their hatred of Roman Catholicism. Roman Catholics drew fresh inspiration from the letter, for the letter, although the warnings were false, gave the Catholics some assurance that there were these about who would bring the Protestant plantation to an end.

A report to the British parliament a few years after the siege, drew the Catholic priests in an unattractive light, a report made after the priests in general had exhorted their flock to arm themselves in the best way possible. Smiths turned out half-pikes and daggers, and women and boys, as well as the men, started to carry weapons. The friars for some reason seemed to be more militant than the ordinary parish priests. As Christians it seems likely that the priests and friars basically wanted peace, and were resorting to recommending violence as a last resort. The priests of the Derry diocese, in the report to parliament, were men of ill character and dissolute life and one was "very offensive to the neighbourhood, for marrying people clandestinely . . ." Shane O'Cahan of Comber was "a most malicious, ill-inclined, dangerous man", whilst James O'Kelly, was "a very weak man". Shane M'Anally of Badony was "a close subtle man"; Bryan O'Cassidy of Ballynascreen, aged fifty, was "cunning and contentious". Neill M'Conway, aged thirty, was "a close subtle fellow and a regular priest", but Murtagh O'Brennan of Magher was "a peaceful man, minding only his meat and his mass".

The majority of Roman Catholics in Ulster had little sympathy for the British position. Under the Catholic dominated corporation, no attempt had been made to persecute Protestants, but fears on the Protestant side were quite kindled when Tyrconnel was made Lord-Deputy of Ireland. Roman Catholics chiefly hated Protestants because of their beliefs, and vice versa, and it was for this

17

B

reason that the Catholics were driven onto the poorer lands. With the accession of James II, Catholics perhaps saw an opportunity of recovering their lands by peaceful means, but the Glorious Revolution of 1688 probably dashed this hope. In later seventeenth century Ulster, Christianity does not appear to have been practised at all.

A lot of double-thinking went on when both sides read their Bibles, that is those that could read. It was difficult to reconcile the Catholic position with the Christian one and that one should "love thy neighbour as thyself". As the one true faith, the Catholic priests must have been aware that their form of Christianity should set an example to the Protestants, whom they regarded as heretics. Roman Catholics, in 1688, denied that they had any animosity towards Protestants, and the priests and bishops, and the Pope, perhaps asserted that it was their mission to peacefully live with Protestants and to accept their lot until Christ and the Virgin Mary dictated otherwise. But Roman Catholics felt persecuted by Protestants as they witnessed the landowners and adventurers arrive from England and Scotland to plant their lands. The scheme that finally emerged in 1609 made room for three types of land grant. The greatest of these was 2,000 acres, the middle grant 1,500 acres, and the smallest 1,000 acres. Roman Catholics were also considered for grants of land provided they gave up their wandering way of life. There were to be three categories of grantee. First there were the undertakers from England and Scotland, who were to pay £5/6s/4d per annum for every thousand acres, and who were permitted to have only Protestant tenants. Next came the servitors, who were to settle the more hostile lands and who were already in the Province. They were permitted to have Irish tenants, but they had to pay a slightly higher head rent. Finally came the Irish who had to pay the highest rent of all — £10/13s/4d per thousand acres. The undertakers had to erect a 'castle' or a bawn upon their territories in a given amount of time. These bawns or walled enclosures would help to protect Protestants during hostile times. A middle holding had to be furnished with a brick or stone house and a bawn. On small holdings the undertaker had to at least build a bawn. All these policies were the brainchild of Arthur Chichester, Lord-Deputy (1604–16), who is regarded as the founder of modern Ulster by Protestants and as a colonialist by Roman Catholics. Chichester was described as "a man of great Honour, Piety, Prudence, Justice, Bounty and Valour . . . so far from Ambition and Covetousness that he neither by his friends nor of himself moved for advancement, Military or Civil, but still it was conferred on him unsought". He had fought in the O'Neill wars, and Roman Catholics regarded him as a monster and a very cruel man. Some see him as a man of great vision, for it is said that he tried to modify the anti-Catholic policies of James I, so that there could be lasting peace in Ireland. His words went unheeded and greedy men were able to impose their will upon Ulster's Roman Catholics. Chichester described the Ulster chieftains' armed retainers as "cruel, wild malefactors and thieves". Those Irish who could not be recruited for service in the army, were to be banished to the wilds of Munster and Connaught. Chichester preferred to see them further afield, and he rounded up 800 or 900 of them who were embarked from Lough Foyle for service in Sweden.

The plantation got off to a good start. Lord Audley applied for fifty great grants, no less than 100,000 acres of Roman Catholic land. His territory was to be divided into thirty-three lots, on which he promised to build a castle and a town for thirty families. There were to be iron mills and glassworks. However Chichester was not impressed with Audley's efforts at plantation in Munster and he only allowed him a single grant of 2,000 acres.

Undertakers came forward eagerly to receive grants in Fermanagh, Donegal, Tyrone, Armagh and Cavan. They fought shy of Derry and County Coleraine as being too hostile a region. North Antrim was left out of the scheme, for here was the seat of the MacDonnell family, Roman Catholics, but good landlords and proving loyal to the Crown. Down and South Antrim were already under control of the Scots. Randal MacDonnell was rewarded for his loyalty and was created Earl of Antrim and was thus left out of the plantation scheme. By 1610 the Scots and English were making their way across the sea to take up their duties in the plantation. Surveyors and map makers set to work in an effort to draw a true and accurate map of the north of Ulster; they always worked with a military escort. Roman Catholics did not want their country mapped and Protestant focused under the leadership of some powerful or popular figures. One consortium was headed by Sir Henry Hobart and included thirteen squires from Norfolk and Suffolk, plus a government official, Richard Harte of Suffolk, whose income was given as £50 per year. One of the Norfolk squires published a pamphlet entitled 'A Direction for the Plantation of Ulster', and was dedicated to the king's eldest son, Prince Henry. The north-west was considered to be barbaric, and County Armagh was preferred, for it was close to the Pale in the event of trouble breaking out. Many of those who settled in Armagh came from Worcestershire. They set out their orchards modelled on those of the Vale of Evesham. The Scots were not afraid of the north-west however, and they tended to be tougher, more determined colonists. Roman Catholics thought them harsh and dour, and in Chichester's words, they started to "hate the Scottyshe deadly".

Chapter 4

A History of Violence

Derry had behind her a history of siege and conflict. It was as if the town, set 120 feet above sea level, was meant to be besieged. In 1609 the planters were laying the foundations of the great siege of 1689. In south-east Ulster, James Hamilton and Hugh Montgomery were pressing ahead with their plans. Clandeboye was the ancestral home of the southern O'Neills, and they were unlucky to have at this time, one Con, a sluggish drunken fellow. There was a drunken brawl between his retainers and the royal troops in Belfast, and as a result Con was arrested. Montgomery promised to use his influence with the king to get him pardoned, but the price of this was to be one half of Con's vast estates. However Montgomery was not to enjoy the fruits of his trickery for long. James Hamilton persuaded King James I that Montgomery's grant was far too large for a single individual.

Hamilton was a true son of the Ayrshire kirk and fellow of the newly-founded Trinity College Dublin. James decreed that Hamilton received one-third of the Clandeboye lands, and Montgomery had to be content with only one-third instead of half, whilst Con was very soon tricked out of what was left of his land by the combined trickery of Hamilton. Montgomery was based at Bangor, where he built a stone house about sixty foot long and twenty-two foot broad. Montgomery, usually on bad terms with Hamilton, settled at Newtownards, where he built the old priory into a mansion. Behind him came Lowland Scottish families such as Boyd, Nevin, Moore, Neil and Catherwood, all receiving large grants of land, both freehold and leasehold, forming the nucleus of a class of yeoman gentry. By 1611, when a government Commission reported on the progress of the plantation, Bangor was a town of eighty new houses, all inhabited by Scots and English. Newtownards was a town of one hundred houses, all peopled by Scots. The houses were of stone or clay, with good roofs, roughcast outside and lime-washed within. They were warm and comfortable and were lived in less than a hundred years ago.

The little ports like Donaghadee and Groomsport developed, and it became easier for the Scots to come to Ulster. There was trade between Portpatrick and Donaghadee when the wind was fair. This close sea link meant that the Scotsman was never far from home. Traders would hire horses at Donaghadee and ride to Newtownards to sell their wares. By evening, traders could be back home at

Lough Ryan. Both Montgomery and Hamilton received peerages in due course, a result of lobbying, according to the Montgomery family historian writing towards the end of the seventeenth century. Hamilton took the title of Viscount Clandeboye and after his death in 1643, his son became Earl of Clanbrassil, a step up the ladder. Montgomery also received a viscountcy and died in 1636. Twenty-five years after his death, his grandson received an earldom, taking the title of Lord Mount-Alexander from the name of his house at Comber. Life was hard outside the little towns for the early settlers, for they had to start from scratch. Virgin land had at first to be cleared of trees and boulders. The soil had to be broken and ploughed, with an eye peeled for the dangerous Irish kern lurking in the woods. The colonists brought with them the present-day Northern Ireland accent. The settlers brought with them their distinctive agricultural implements, and these have survived. The Ulster spade has a very long handle for extra leverage, and a longer blade than an English spade. The Ulster spade was well suited for delving the rich moist earth or for carving out pieces of turf from the bogs. These implements were at length manufactured in spade mills. A belief sprang up that a Protestant dug with a different blade than a Catholic, an Ulster shibboleth — "Which foot does he dig with?"

The happiest part of Ulster in those days, according to the Montgomery historian, was County Down. Montgomery of Braidstones had an enterprising wife, Elizabeth Shaw. We hear that there was ". . . occasion to Sir Hugh's lady to build water mills in all the parishes to the great advantage of her house . . . the millers also prevented the necessity of bringing meal from Scotland and grinding with quairn stones (as the Irish did to make their graddon) both which inconveniences the people at their first coming were forced to undergo . . . She easily got men for plough and barn, for many came over who had not stocks to plant and take leases of land but had brought a cow or two and a few sheep, for which she gave them grass and so much grain per annum and a horse and a garden plot to live on and some land for flax and potatoes . . . and this was but part of her good management, for she set up and encouraged linen and woollen manufactory, which soon brought down the prices of breakens and narrow cloths of both sort".

A picture is drawn that everyone minded their trade, plough and spade; orchards and gardens were planted. Everyone was "innocently busy". There was "no strife, contention, querulous lawyers or Scottish or Irish feuds between clans and families and surnames, disturbing the tranquillity of those times; and the towns and temples were erected with other great works". However most of Ulster was still infested with Irish swordsmen and Chichester had only managed to transport a fraction of them to Sweden. They took to the forests as outlaws and made attacks upon the planters as outlaws. They were human wolves, and manhunts were organized to slay them.

The undertakers had at first shown little enthusiasm for the Derry and Coleraine regions. Here the warlike O'Cahans were on the prowl and memories were fresh for O'Dogherty's destruction of Derry. Sir Cahir O'Dogherty was a young chieftain of Inishowen, who had been treated with kindness by Docwra, so much so that O'Dogherty treated Docwra as a father. He had stood loyally by his patron throughout the Tyrone wars and he had been knighted by Mountjoy, the then Lord-Deputy, for fighting by Docwra's side at a battle at Augher. But now O'Dogherty was deprived of his lands by the government, and he was a man with a grievance. An unsuccessful attempt was made to seize O'Dogherty's castle at Birt in his absence. It was said that Paulet, the Vice-Provost, had gone so far as to strike Sir Cahir with his whip. Paulet was a self-opinionated young bully, who was detested by his troops, but he had good connections. Sir Cahir invited Henry Hart, the Governor of Culmore, to a friendly dinner party, with the object of kidnapping him. By threatening to kill him, he persuaded Hart's wife to persuade the Culmore garrison to open the gates on the pretext that the Governor was lying outside with a broken leg. The O'Dogherties seized the fort, giving Sir Cahir a useful stock of small arms and ammunition, several cannon and two sailing boats which had been drawn up on the beaches below. O'Dogherty now marched through the night to Derry, arriving there at two o'clock in the morning, to find the town peacefully asleep. The walls had not yet been built and Derry was only defended by a ditch and bank.

O'Dogherty broke in and the Inishowen clans yelled in the streets. Some made a flight for it, including Paulet, but he was killed at Ensign Corbet's house to which he had managed to reach. Corbet was slain and his wife slew her husband's slayer, only to be cut down herself. Lieutenant Gordon rushed naked from his house, armed only with a sword, and managed to kill two of the enemy before he was stunned by a stone and hacked to bits. Lieutenant Baker took command of the garrison, concentrating them upon the sheriff's and the bishop's house.

When the Irish attacked from Culmore, he surrendered with a promise of a safe conduct for himself and his men. The promise was kept and Hart of Culmore and his wife were also set free. The Catholics set fire to Derry, throwing most of the guns into the Foyle, and taking Lady Paulet and Mrs Montgomery, they withdrew into the north-west.

Sir Cahir wandered aimlessly about Ulster for a few months without gaining any important allies. He was hunted down and killed and his head sent to adorn a spike over one of the gates of Dublin. A story goes that he was starved to death in his castle at Buncrana. The two English ladies were released, but despite the English victory, Docwra's Derry had been, for all intents and purposes, destroyed. Only the cathedral and the stone chimneys of the houses survived the fire. However this was only the beginning for Derry, for it was never again to be taken by an enemy. The Irish Solicitor General, surveying the ruins in 1609, said that "it was the fairest-begun city that ever was made in so short a time, and so well seated upon a goodly river; but now all is wasted, save only the rampiers of the fort; and it is hardly to be brought to its former goodness unless some great man, who shall be lord of O'Dogherty's country, shall make his principal residence there. In the meantime it is a place of little strength and lies at the mercy of any that will attempt to seize it".

The Protestants of Londonderry, in December 1688, would not listen to their Bishop, Ezekiel Hopkins, to keep the gates of the city open. The Protestants were certain that the Catholics would massacre them, after the style of 1641. The appearance of 'the Comber letter' had not helped matters. Copies of the letter were quickly made and circulated. Reports of the letter reached Tyrconnel in Dublin, and he assured some leading Protestants that it was a confounded lie. Many however took an assurance from Tyrconnel that it was false as an indication that the letter was true. Tyrconnel hurled his wig into the fire, along with his hat, as lying Dick was wont to do on occasions that annoyed him.

In County Derry, George Canning of Garvagh got a copy of 'the Comber letter' from a friend in Belfast and at once sent a copy to Alderman Tomkin of Londonderry and another to George Phillips in Newtownlimavady. Meanwhile the Earl of Antrim's regiment was nearing Derry, all this taking place on 6th December. The appearance of the untrained Redshanks was however quite daunting as they marched along, if marching is the right word to describe the force. Antrim's force was over 1,200 strong, as against the 400 Londonderry had been prepared for. Behind the regiment was a rabble of women and boys, for the force was expecting spoil. Mackenzie, the Presbyterian minister of Cookstown said that the men were "rake-hells" and the women "vultures". Dr King, who two years later became Bishop of Derry, said that the men were a pack of ruffians, many of the captains and officers being familiar to them, since they had been in jail in the town for thefts and robberies. The army came down over the hills from Coleraine and into Limavady on what was known as 'the Murder-Hole Road'. Antrim billeted himself for the night upon George Phillips, who lived in a house at the head of Main Street, and was the town's leading citizen. Phillips was even older than the Earl, for he was in his eighty-ninth year. He had been Governor of Londonderry, and despite his age, he was quite witty.

The Redshanks stalked the streets of Limavady, alarming old Phillips. He sent a messenger riding through the night to Londonderry, which was only seventeen miles away. He wanted his friend Alderman Norman to consult the responsible people of the town about letting such a rabble as Antrim's within the city gates. So alarmed was he that he sent another rider early next morning to warn Norman to close the gates of Derry, promising the citizens that he would join them next day and stand by them in all eventualities.

The first of Phillips's messengers arrived on the morning of 7th December at the very moment Alderman Tomkins was reading out his copy of 'the Comber letter' to a group of worried citizens. They became further worried when they realized the danger of admitting Antrim's troops, and they did not know what to do. The news of the Redshanks seemed to confirm their worst fears, that 'the Comber letter' was genuine and that 1641 had arrived again. It seemed that the Redshanks had come close to slaughtering them, for 'the Comber letter' had said that the massacre would start in two days' time. Protestants in Londonderry therefore would appear to be the first victims of the massacre.

To refuse entry to the troops acting under Tyrconnel's orders, would be an act of treason, for Lying Dick was the Lord-Deputy of James II, God's anointed, and still the only lawful king. Mountjoy, who had been called South, was still firm in his allegiance to James, and the habit of loyalty to the king was deeply engrained. The penalties for treason were great — the gallows, the disembowelling knife and the quartering block. Mountjoy had advised Enniskillen — a strong Protestant town — to submit to James's authority, and assured them that the king would protect them and that there was no possibility of a massacre. Phillips's second messenger arrived in the city just as Tomkins and his friends were still undecided and anxiously debating. The messenger said that he had passed Antrim's vanguard only two miles from the city. They would still have to cross the Foyle from the Waterside by boat, for there was no bridge.

The whole burden of making a decision fell upon Tomkins, who now sought advice from leaders of the Church. James Gordon, Presbyterian minister of Glendermot, on the Waterside, exclaimed that the gates should be shut. The Church of Ireland Bishop, Ezekiel Hopkins said that the people of Derry should be loyal to their sovereign and that rebellion was a serious matter. The younger men started to call for action, and they were secretly supported by their elders. Horace Kennedy, one of the sheriffs, was one of those who hinted to the Apprentice Boys, that Antrim's regiment should be kept out and that the gates should be shut.

The watchers on the walls now caught sight of the Redshanks, for they had reached the Waterside and were beginning to cross the Foyle in boats. Two of their officers swaggered up to the gates, and they gained admittance, presenting their warrant. They demanded quarters for their men and forage for their horses. A technical defect in the warrant enabled the sheriffs to hesitate further, but now the Apprentice Boys took the law into their own hands. There were thirteen altogether: Henry Campsie, William Crookshanks, Robert Sherrard, Daniel Sherrard, Alexander Irwin, James Steward, Robert Morrison, Alexander Cunningham, Samuel Hunt, James Spike, John Cunningham, William Cairns and Samuel Harvey.

These names have never been forgotten in Ulster, for the young men drew their swords at midday on 7th December 1688 and ran to the mainguard and seized the keys. They rushed down to Ferryquay Gate to raise the drawbridge and close the gates in the face of Antrim's men, who were only sixty yards away. A citizen, James Morrison, shouted to the astonished Redshanks from the walls, that they should retreat. When the Redshanks refused to shift, Morrison shouted out that someone should bring a "great gun" to convince Antrim's men. The Redshanks then retreated to their boats, returning to the Waterside, where they assaulted the inhabitants of the suburb, so annoyed were they at not being admitted. So Derry had been saved for the Protestant cause.

Chapter 5

The Rebellion of 1641

The Protestants had closed the gates of Londonderry because they feared a repetition of the Catholic massacres of 1641. As with the closing of the gates, the great rebellion started in a simple way. On Sunday, 24th October 1641, in the tiny village of Derrykeighan on the north Antrim coast, Protestants were at their morning service. The door of the little church burst open and Archibald Stewart of Ballintoy rushed up the aisle and into the pulpit to warn the congregation that the Irish had risen in rebellion in the south of County Londonderry. Moneymore had fallen into their hands and it was anyone's guess what would happen in the rest of the county. Archibald at this point did not know that the Catholics had captured and burnt Desertmartin and Magherafelt. He ordered the people of Derrykeighan to arm themselves and post garrisons in strong points in the region. It seemed as if this was no disorganized rising, but an organized rebellion that was soon to engulf Ulster and the rest of Ireland.

The scenes at Derrykeighan church would be repeated all over the Province. The rising had long been foretold by the authorities. William Rowley rode through the night from Moneymore to bring the news to Coleraine, and a flood of refugees poured into the town that Sunday, 24th October 1641.

The barony of Loughinsolin fell to the Catholics. They seized Dungannon and the neighbouring forests of Mountjoy and Charlemont. The clans were overrunning Cavan and Enniskillen. The O'Cahans of the Roe Valley, the MacDonnells, McAlisters, O'Hagans and McMullans of North Antrim were on the prowl. The warnings of Chichester and others had gone unheeded, and the English were mystified by the Irish attitude to their civilization. Clarendon, who ten years later wrote a *"History of the Rebellion and Civil Wars in Ireland"*, said that English rule brought peace and security to Ireland, and that both Roman Catholics and Protestants worked together during the reign of James I, and that this situation was built upon during the reign of Charles I. The wealth of Ireland was increased under English rule and several new industries were introduced. The land was generally improved, by introducing good husbandry.

By 1641, Ireland had made a spectacular recovery from the devastations of the Tyrone wars. When the Papal Nuncio, Rinuccini arrived in Ireland with money, arms and ammunition for the rebels, his secretary, Dr Massari, in a letter to his brother in Florence, described the country between Kenmare and

25

Killarney as full of rich pastures and livestock, especially cattle and sheep. He wrote that food was abundant and that the people eat well. They constantly make toasts, the usual drink being Spanish wine, French claret, good beer and excellent milk. Butter was plentiful with all kinds of food and there was plenty of apples, pears, plums and artichokes. All food was cheap, and a fat ox cost sixteen shillings, a sheep fifteen pence, a pair of capons or fowls five pence; eggs a farthing each. A good sized fish cost a penny, and both salt and freshwater fish were cheap. A thousand pilchards and oysters cost twenty-five baiocchi. Horses were numerous, strong, well built and swift. For five pounds it was possible to buy a nag, which in Italy would not be got for over one hundred gold pieces.

The sense of injustice was strongest in Ulster, despite the good times under Britain. The land confiscations of the start of the century were still bitterly remembered. The old Irish had lost great possessions.

The rest of Ireland also was full of discontent. The Catholic lords and gentry were alarmed at the policies of Laud and the growing strength of the Puritan movement in England. The English were determined to introduce their own laws and methods of administration for the old Gaelic practises and customs. The seeds of rebellion were sown by the foolish policies of the young Earl of Antrim, Randal MacDonnell, who had been brought up in the English court. He was "frivolous, irresponsible and very good looking", and Charles I, charmed by this Irishman, bestowed upon him the peninsula of Kintyre, which for a generation had been the de facto possession of the strong Protestant Clan Campbell. They were determined not to be dispossessed by the Catholic MacDonnells from across the North Channel. However, Randal MacDonnell was equally determined to enter upon his new inheritance, and towards the end of 1638, he asked the Lord-Deputy to help arm him with a view to an attack upon the Campbells.

The Lord-Deputy was Thomas Wentworth, who refused the request, considering Randal an incompetent fellow. A few months later the Earl of Antrim was putting forward even wilder suggestions. He appeared in Dublin, just at the moment when war was about to break out between Scotland and England. Antrim said that he was the king's champion and that he was going to build a fleet and raise an army of over 10,000 men, which he proposed to take to Scotland. He would teach the Scots to be obedient to their king with the help of his great friend Phelim O'Neill. Antrim said that he and his friend should be knighted for these services, and Wentworth agreed.

Towards the end of 1639, Charles, beset by problems in Scotland and in parliament, recalled Wentworth. Wentworth had raised a considerable Irish army, and by 1640, in a brief visit to Dublin, its strength was raised to 9,000 men. He was now Earl of Strafford. However he was accused of conspiring against the king to use the Irish army against England, and he went to the block in May 1641. His Irish army was disbanded. This army was scattered throughout the country. The troops fraternized with the 'wild Irish', distributing their equipment to them. Catholics in Ireland saw that if the Puritan movement in England gained the upper hand, it would spell trouble for the old religion, with the strict enforcement of the penal laws. The circumstances were never so favourable for revolt, and from the start the 1641 rebellion seems to have been well organized and the secret well kept. It was intended to seize strongholds not only in Ulster, but also Dublin Castle, together with leading members of the king's government in Ireland. However an informer let go the secret of the plans in his cups, and the attack on Dublin Castle had to be called off. In Ulster it was a different story. Here bonfires blazed from the hilltops, telling the story of the success of the revolt, and calling the clansmen to arms. The colonists' farmsteads were going up in flames, whilst the Irish drove off the cattle. Newry fell; eastern Ulster was in a state of terror. Belfast was threatened.

The colonists tried to fight a defensive action from behind their castles and bawns. Sir Phelim O'Neill, reported to be at the head of 20,000 men, led the rebellion. He said that he had taken up arms to free his king from the shackles of the Parliamentarians, and that he was no traitor. He flourished what he said was a commission under the King's Great Seal, which authorized him to seize castles and other properties. Copies of Sir Phelim's commission were soon being circulated throughout Ireland, and many believed it to be genuine, but the king's reputation suffered at the hands of Sir Phelim.

Autumn passed into Winter, and the rebellion made great headway in the North. The planters would not trust any Irishman. Manus O'Cahan was put in command of Dungiven Castle, for it was thought that he was loyal. He forgot about the hardship his clan had suffered at the hands of the British. However, he soon joined the rebels and showed himself to be a cruel man. James Farrell, at Ballykelly, soon deserted to the Catholic cause, killing a number of English before he did so. Shortly before Christmas, an Irish army of about 2,000 men approached the little plantation town of Garvagh in mid-Derry. The Protestants marched out to meet them, led by Edward Rowley and William Canning. They were defeated at Revelyn's Hill. Both Canning and Rowley were killed.

The planters at Garvagh fled north to Coleraine, where the earth walls were manned by 650 men organized into eight companies, which was reduced to seven, for one of the companies was mostly Catholic. Coleraine was packed with refugees, little huts being erected to house them, whilst some of the Protestants were lodged in the church. The Mayor wrote to Dublin in January 1642, asking for arms, food and pay for his troops. To save accommodation and food, he shipped 3,000 women and children to Scotland; but this did not prevent an outbreak of plague in the Spring. The plague raged for four months and killed 2,000 people, and the dead were buried so close together, that they resembled packed herrings.

Fourteen miles west of Coleraine, the castles of Limavady and Ballycastle (not to be confused with the Antrim coast town) were still intact, and were commanded by the brothers Dudley and Thomas Phillips, the sons of old Sir Thomas. In March 1642 they reported to Dublin that the colonists were being murdered daily, and that the better sort were fleeing to Londonderry and

Coleraine. There were about 1,300 people, making up the population of Limavady and Ballycastle, but only about 300 of these were fit to bear arms. Many of the others were women and children, who consumed much of the food. They dared not go from one castle to the other without a great guard, or fetch water without great danger. They were eating one meal per day, and they expected that they could hold out for two months. They put in an urgent request for arms, ammunition and pay for the soldiers, and salves and ointments for the many wounded.

The Mayor of Londonderry, too, was writing to Dublin. He said that there were great miseries daily affecting them, and that there were so many poor people crowded into the city and that famine and plague would kill them if the Catholics' swords did not. Ships were carrying people to Scotland. The Mayor of Londonderry wrote to Dublin and said that "the terror of the rebellion hath struck such a feare in the British of these partes that their hartes are gone and therefore it is too little purpose to stay their bodies".

Two Lord Justices, Sir John Borlase and Sir William Parsons, carried on the king's government in Dublin. They made some attempt to respond to the appeals from the North, and managed to send Dudley Phillips, in Limavady, two barrels of powder, forty barrels of herrings and twelve barrels of beef. The rebellion had now spread to other parts of Ireland, for the O'Neills were besieging Monaghan, the O'Byrnes were on the rampage in Wicklow, and in Munster Lord Muskerry deserted to the Irish. In the early Summer of 1642, it seemed possible that the Ulster rising might be contained.

In the fertile Laggan district in eastern Donegal, two professional soldiers, Sir William Stewart and his brother Sir Robert, raised a volunteer force out of the Scots who had colonized the area. The Lagganers moved quickly to the help of other Protestants, for they recaptured Strabane, relieved the Phillips brothers in Limavady and then moved down into the Magilligan peninsula, where they slaughtered 300 Irish. They then marched up the Roe Valley to the Gelvin burn, only a few miles from Dungiven, where they were confronted by 3,500 O'Cahan and their allies. The O'Cahans fought well, but at length they turned and fled. Dungiven Castle was recaptured and the rebel Manus O'Cahan sent to jail in Londonderry. The Lagganers now turned north again to relieve Coleraine, destroying all the corn on the way that might not be of use to the British. They then marched home to Donegal, having inspired great terror amongst the Irish.

Powerful aid had come from Scotland for the planters. The Scottish government hated everything Catholic and wanted to help their kith and kin in Ulster. In the Spring of 1642 they despatched an army of several thousand men under command of a professional soldier, Major General Robert Monro, who was to prove quite ruthless. He recaptured Newry, and hung sixty citizens and two priests, and it was only at the intervention of more humane counsel, that prevented him executing all his women prisoners. The forces of law and order, with the arrival of the Earl of Leven to Ulster, amounted to 20,000 men. Leven did not remain long in Ireland, but Monro remained for many years. The Ulster rebels had concentrated their efforts upon the English settlers, in the meanwhile leaving the Scots alone, perhaps because they were greater in numbers. Scots' hatred of the Irish perhaps prompted a garrison to strike at the peninsula of Island Magee, which lay between Larne Lough and the sea, in January 1642. The English and Scots murdered in one night all the inhabitants, which numbered above 3,000 men, women and children. The Catholics were driven over the Gobbins cliffs into the sea and the name of Slaughterford Bridge at the southern end of Island Magee, recalls the event.

Civil war had now broken out in England, and Ireland was reduced to a state of great misery and confusion. At least five different factions maintained armies in the field at the same time: there were the Catholic rebels, led by Owen Roe O'Neill, who had joined them from Scotland, and a relative of the great O'Neill. There were the Catholic "Lords of the Pale", who had at first sided with the rebels, but who declared that they would support King Charles if he would give them freedom of religion and power for themselves. There was the Marquess of Ormonde, leading a second Royalist group, who was unconditionally loyal to the Crown; he was the King's Viceroy. The Ulster colonists split into Royalist and Roundhead, having at first presented a united front against the Irish. Monro's Scottish army continued to distinguish itself with atrocities, but it was beaten by Owen Roe O'Neill at the Battle of Benburb. The Scots in Ireland at first supported the English parliament, and then turned Royalist when Scotland changed sides. Derry, which at one time was held for parliament by Sir Charles Coote, was besieged by a combined force of Monro's Scots and Ormonde's Royalists, but was relieved by Owen Roe O'Neill and his Catholics.

The war dragged on for twelve years. Sir William Petty, when he surveyed the country for the Cromwellian Settlement, estimated that out of Ireland's population of 1,466,000, at least 616,000 had perished. Those last resistance was stamped out in 1653, and lay helpless at the feet of the English conquerors. Cromwell himself arrived in Ireland in 1649, determined to avenge the Protestant dead. This he did at Drogheda and again at Wexford. The Irish never forgot Drogheda, but the colonists in the North remembered 1641. It was reckoned that within the first two or three days of the rebellion, that at least 40 and 50,000 Ulster Protestants were slaughtered. An Irish historian, William Curry, said that 150,000 Protestants were massacred in cold blood in the first two months of the rebellion. George Walker, when he preached in Londonderry during the siege said that 200,000 Protestants had perished. Others put figures as low as 2,109 after the first two years of the rebellion. On evidence given by other Protestants the figure stands at 1,619 more.

Chapter 6

Aftermath of the Closing of the Gates

The heroes of the hour were the thirteen Apprentice Boys, who closed the gates of Bishop's Gate in the face of the Earl of Antrim, a Catholic leading a substantial army. He called for the citizens to surrender, but the Apprentice Boys shouted "No surrender!". They were reflecting the popular mood of the city, but history sees them as being extreme. Any attempt to gain admittance to Londonderry forcibly, would be inadvisable. Antrim did not want to start a civil war, so he withdrew to Coleraine, collecting his scattered regiment together. Meanwhile Phillips accepted the Governorship of Derry, which he had last held in the early days of Charles II's reign.

However, the Apprentice Boys only reflected one shade of opinion, for there were others in the city who wanted appeasement, and they gathered in the market place. Cormac O'Neill, Mayor of Londonderry, was absent on military service in Tyrconnel's army, so it was left to John Buchanan, to win the citizens back to allegiance to King James. Alderman Gervais Squire called Buchanan a traitor to his face, and was followed by Bishop Ezekiel Hopkins, who warned of the dangers of not obeying their lawful sovereign. He said that the citizens would bring a war upon themselves and that Tyrconnel was the king's lawful deputy in Ireland. Those who resist James would be resisting God, and that a great army would come to Ireland, which would destroy Derry. There would be great violence and the city would lose all its wealth. Hopkins exhorted the citizens to submit to the present powers. At this moment the Apprentice Boy Alexander Irwin was reported to have shouted from the crowd that no one should listen to the bishop. The citizens decided not to heed Hopkins.

The closing of the gates had acted like magic and had aroused the citizens to defend their city. Bishop Hopkins dissociated himself from this act of treason and withdrew to Raphoe a few days later. It is claimed that Hopkins was what the Apprentice Boy Irwin said he was "a traitor, ready to sell out at the first moment", but many of his predictions came true: great havoc came to Derry and a great army came into the land. Hopkins was only putting into words what most of the responsible citizens were thinking, and it is easy to malign him in retrospect. An act of rebellion was a very serious matter, as he had told Alderman Tomkins, and Londonderry was in no state to withstand attack. Mackenzie says that at this time there were less than 300 men fit to bear arms. Most of the arms were not in good condition and the cannon was unmounted. There were no provisions in store and only six barrels of powder; or according to Walker's account, only two.

Hopkins had long believed in passive obedience to royal power, an idea he had expounded in Christ Church, Dublin, in 1669, on the twentieth anniversary of Charles I's execution. He had said that "If the supreme Majesty should abuse his sovereign power and command thee to do what God his superior hath commanded thee not to do, *thou art not to resist,* nor to raise tumults and seditions to depose him from his authority, but only quietly and meekly to appeal unto God, who alone is his judge". The Presbyterian Joseph Boyce has looked favourably upon Hopkins, despite the fact that Hopkins advised the citizens to open the gates after the Apprentice Boys had closed them. He said that Hopkins should not be branded ". . . as one of Tyrconnel's agents or a well-wisher to the Irish and Papal interest . . ." There is no evidence that Hopkins was a supporter of James, and that he was merely advocating his policy of "passive obedience". It is almost certain that he swore allegiance to King William, for in an Act of Attainder, passed by James's Dublin parliament a few months later, his name appears amongst those who fermented rebellion and treason. His income was confiscated by James, and until his death in 1690, he earned a modest living as a vicar in London. He had been highly esteemed for his intellect and learning in Londonderry. This has not prevented Presbyterian writers condemning and making fun of Hopkins. They paint him as a timorous creature in comparison to James Gordon, the Presbyterian minister, who advised Tomkins to close the gates. However when the siege started, neither James Gordon or the Apprentice Boy Irwin were to be found within the walls.

Gordon was a disreputable character and had tried to commit a 'deed of rapt' against the person of one Helen Gordon; for this, in 1667, he was expelled from his Scottish living by the Synod of Moray. He obtained another living in Scotland from which he was deposed, for swearing, drinking, striking and lying. There were strong rumours of sexual misconduct, and in 1680 he admitted fornication with his domestic servant, named Sivewright. The Moderator passed upon him the sentence of 'Lesser Excommunication', upon which he promptly emigrated to Ulster, to obtain a living at Bovevagh in County Londonderry, but he was soon expelled by the Presbytery of Coleraine. But he was able to obtain yet another living at Glendermot, and how he did this remains a mystery. At this point he wanted to become a government spy and he pulled many strings to obtain this ambition. Bishop Hopkins was asked by the Archbishop of Armagh to enquire into his character, and Hopkins concluded that Gordon wanted to become a spy because of the money. Hopkins strongly advised against his employment. Ormond, then the Lord Lieutenant had agreed; he said that Gordon led a ". . . vagabond course of life . . ." But Gordon was able to survive his wickedness and died as minister of Cardross, in Dumbartonshire.

The 9th December, the day appointed for the massacre of Protestants by 'the

Comber letter', came around. The Catholics had now left Derry, and the city was safe. Antrim's Redshanks had retreated and every gate was manned by a Protestant guard. Macaulay says that throughout the length of Ireland every large Protestant home became a fortress and that armed men were watching and lights burned from early sunset to late sunrise. Few went to bed that night. Midnight came, but there was no massacre. There was great relief in Londonderry now that the Protestants were to be spared, but the city had defied King James and it was too late to turn back. Alderman Norman and his friends wrote to Mountjoy, who had now reached Dublin, to represent their case to Tyrconnel in a favourable light. They blamed the rabble in the town, saying that the better sort could not restrain them. They said that they hoped that Tyrconnel would look upon what had been done as a great service to him, and that the king would likewise look at the closing of the gates as an act of loyalty, in view of the fact that the Protestants thought there would be a massacre. They also wrote to the Irish Society in London, saying that it was the youths that had closed the gates and that they could not persuade them otherwise. However opinion within Derry was hardening. John Campsie, the Mayor of the former Protestant Corporation, had resumed office, and he and the sheriffs published a declaration praising the action of the Apprentice Boys. It ended saying that "We have resolved to stand upon our guard and to defend our walls, and not to admit of any Papists whatsoever to quarter amongst us". The few Catholics that remained were expelled from the city and a convent of Dominican friars ejected.

In the previous weeks there had been an exodus of Protestants, and there were few men suitable to man the walls. Most of the 300 fit men lacked all military training. However news of Londonderry's plight soon spread, and reinforcements came streaming in from the countryside. Captain John Forward came in from Donegal, together with William Stewart with 2 or 300 horsemen. From St Johnston, a few miles upstream from the city, came John Cowan, bringing a company of infantry. Forward had disregarded Dublin's orders to disarm the Donegal Protestants, and he had kept a shipload of arms and powder from Holland, which Derry later used. David Cairns, a Derry lawyer, rode to the city from his country house in Tyrone, to praise the action of the Apprentice Boys, one of whom was his nephew. He then proceeded to form the city into a garrison, with six companies, each with a captain, a lieutenant and an ensign. Five of the original Apprentice Boys, Crookshanks, Irwin, Morrison, Sherrard and Cunningham, were appointed lieutenants, but by the time of the siege, there was a completely different set of officers. Cairns then sailed to England with the city's appeal to the Irish Society. He promised to do his best to obtain arms and ammunition, he was equipped with a 'private key' so that he could carry on secret correspondence.

Tyrconnel, upon hearing of Derry's rebellion, having stamped on his wig and thrown it into the fire, sent Mountjoy back northwards with six companies of his regiment to reoccupy the city. The troops had only been in Dublin for three days on their long march south; now they would have to start the long march north. A few days before Christmas they reached Omagh, where Mountjoy learned that the Catholic Corporation in the city had been ousted, and that the leadership of Londonderry had fallen to old Colonel Phillips and the members of the former Protestant Corporation. They sent spokesmen to parley with Mountjoy, emphasizing their loyalty to James but saying that under no circumstances would Catholic soldiers be allowed into the city.

It was eventually agreed that Mountjoy's two companies, all of them Protestant, would be allowed into Londonderry, under command of Lieutenant Colonel Robert Lundy, also a Protestant. Colonel Phillips at once resigned his office and Mountjoy appointed Lundy, Military Governor of Londonderry. Mountjoy, against the advice of many of his friends, returned to Dublin, at the same time that news arrived that King James had fled his kingdom, and was now a refugee at the Court of King Louis XIV. The king had a reputation for bravery, but not now. As William of Orange advanced from the West Country, James's nerve had left him. He had advanced from Salisbury to meet his son-in-law, but had turned back because his nose was continually bleeding. He described England as being a poisoned nation, and was wary of John Churchill, who had defected and whom he thought had intended to kidnap him. James fell back upon London and allowed William of Orange's Dutch troops to occupy the capital. James showed much indecision, and this it has been said, was due to his obsession with his sexual sins, which were many. He wrote later that the hated himself because of this. At length James escaped from his kingdom upon a second attempt. He had William's connivance and he joined his wife and the baby Prince of Wales in France. He at once set about trying to recover his throne with great energy; if he had done this earlier it would have made flight unnecessary. History has called the bloodless revolution which ousted James, 'The Glorious Revolution'.

Tyrconnel was loyal to James, and he saw that war between England and Ireland would spell disaster for the smaller island. Tyrconnel wrote a letter to his king to inform him of the position the revolution put Ireland in. Mountjoy was asked to take the letter to France; he suggested it might be better to choose a Catholic. The Lord-Deputy reacted violently to this suggestion in words not fit to repeat. Tyrconnel seems now to have doubted Mountjoy's loyalty, and by sending him to France, he was putting him out of harm's way. Upon leaving Derry for the second time. Mountjoy had ordered the garrison's guns to be mounted on their carriages, the guns repaired and all other measures taken for the city's safety.

Sending Mountjoy to France seems a nasty course of action taken by the Lord-Deputy. Stephen Rice the Chief Baron of the Exchequer accompanied Mountjoy to Paris with a secret letter informing James that Mountjoy was a traitor and that Ireland was staunchly Jacobite and would rise at the king's command. To James's credit, he was prepared to let Mountjoy return to Ireland, but Louis XIV had him sent to the Bastille, from which he was released after three years in time to die for William on the field of Steenkirk. Irish Jacobites praised Tyrconnel's action as a crafty move to get Mountjoy out of the way in

33

C

case he might lead Ireland's Protestants. Is it any wonder that Protestants called Tyrconnel 'Lying Dick Talbot', for little faith could be put upon his word.

In London, William of Orange and his adviser sat waiting to see which side Lying Dick would fall. They were not aware that Stephen Rice had taken to Paris an even more secret message. If James did not back Tyrconnel, then the Lord-Deputy would make Ireland a province of France. This is what Avaux, the French ambassador in Ireland reported to James a few months later.

Tyrconnel stood in high regard in royal circles; it was certain that he would be loyal to James, but in actual fact, he changed his mind. He was all for sending Hamilton to Ireland to offer generous terms to the Irish Catholics. He failed in his mission, nor did he return to England, as he had promised. It seems that Hamilton had no intention of trying to change Tyrconnel's mind. Macaulay conjectures that Hamilton had wanted to keep his promise to William but found this to be beyond him, and that Tyrconnel had genuinely wanted to come to terms with the Prince of Orange, but now found the Irish in a revengeful mood. The Irish did not like Tyrconnel corresponding with James, and they threatened to burn Tyrconnel's palace down with him in it if he was going to make terms with William. The Lord-Deputy and Hamilton swam with the tide.

Hamilton was put in command of an army to subdue Ulster. This was too much for Hamilton's sponsor, young John Temple, who flung himself into the River Thames. Macaulay says that William had the last word about Hamilton's treachery, who at the Battle of the Boyne thought little about Hamilton's honour.

Chapter 7

Lying Dick Talbot

Tyrconnel played a dominant role in Irish affairs over a five-year period, and probably no man more than he did more to harden Protestant attitudes in Ulster by his uncompromising Catholic policies. He came of old Anglo-Norman stock and was the only lieutenant to survive the massacre of Drogheda thirty years before. He was the youngest of sixteen children of William Talbot and Alison Netterville. The Talbots were one of the most ancient families of the British Isles, at the head of which stood England's senior earl, Lord Shrewsbury. The Leinster branch of the family had been given the castle and lordship of Malahide by Henry II. His father was a successful lawyer who became Recorder of Dublin; but had to be removed from that office because on the accession of James I, as a good Catholic, he had refused to take the Oath of Supremacy. He never compromised over his religion, but he quickly made his peace with James and received a grant of land and a baronetcy, after which he ceased to criticize the government.

William Talbot died when Richard was only four. Richard was brought up at the family seat at Carton in County Kildare by his eldest brother. By 1647 Richard, then only seventeen, was to be seen fighting as a cornet of horse in the army of the Lords of the Pale. A year or two later, after having survived the Drogheda massacre, he again escaped with his life when he fell into the hands of Charles Coote, a hot-headed and bloody man, but he was saved by an exchange of prisoners. By 1656 he had joined Charles II in exile at Antwerp. Charles II described all the Talbots as "naughty fellows . . . ". Richard's brother, Peter, was a Jesuit priest and a born intriguer, who was distrusted by nearly everyone who knew him. Clarendon wanted Peter Talbot "sent to a remote convent and kept close from further activity". However Charles's brother James, then Duke of York, formed a high opinion of Richard Talbot, from which he did not waver over a friendship that lasted over thirty years. Lying Dick became a member of James's household in exile, first as a gentleman of the bedchamber and then as a Lieutenant Colonel in the Duke of York's regiment. Clarendon said that Talbot owed his quick promotion because "he was (a) very handsome young man, wore good clothes, and was without doubt of a clear ready courage, which was virtue enough to recommend a man to the Duke's good opinion". Talbot boasted that it was he — Richard — that had converted the Duke of York to Roman Catholicism, and if this is so, it was to strengthen the bond between them.

35

In 1655, Talbot was involved in a plot to murder Oliver Cromwell. Macaulay has not a good word to say about Tyrconnel, who described the plan as 'infamous', but at this time political assassination was regarded as a legitimate weapon and one which the English had employed against dangerous Irishmen who had taken refuge in Europe. Talbot was very brave, for no one but a brave man would have entered the England of the Lord Protector's Major Generals. He was betrayed by a double agent and he escaped with his life. Talbot was interrogated by Cromwell himself, who threatened to put him on the rack, but Talbot said that he could tell Cromwell nothing: "I have nothing to confess and can only invent lies". Talbot was not subjected to torture and he was at length able to intoxicate Cromwell's gaolers with his last twenty pounds, whilst he slipped down to the Thames on a cord, where a boat had been prepared for him. He was ten days at sea, landing at Calais, still nailed and shut up between some boards of the boat.

With the Restoration, Talbot returned to London in the company of the Duke of York. We hear of him involved in a plot to discredit Anne Hyde, the elder Clarendon's daughter, with the object of freeing James from his engagement with her, for the Duke of York had already seduced and made the girl pregnant. Talbot was said to have been one of four courtiers who came forward to declare that Anne was unsuitable to marry James in view of her conduct with them. Nevertheless, James and Anne did get married, and both remained on good terms with Lying Dick, so Anne must have had a very forgiving nature or Talbot was not involved in the plot to discredit her. Talbot remained at court as chief pander to James, a notorious womanizer, who had one affair after the other, and Talbot was looked upon as the manager of these intrigues. Talbot, during these years, was acting as the London agent for the Irish Catholics who were trying to recover their estates under the involved procedures of the Acts of Settlement. He worked on commission; although he never seemed greedy for money, he laid the foundations of a sizeable fortune. When the Protestant reaction set in, his activities laid him open to attack. 1673, the House of Commons petitioned Charles II that Colonel Richard Talbot, should be immediately dismissed from all commands either civil or military and forbidden all access to court. The Commons also asked for the banishment of Peter Talbot, pretended Archbishop of Dublin, for his notorious disloyalty and disobedience and contempt of laws.

Talbot made himself scarce, first in France, then in Yorkshire, and only returned to Ireland when the gentlemanly Ormonde had again become Lord Lieutenant. His move to Ireland was ill-timed, for Talbot was arrested, Protestant enemies exultant at his downfall, but the gloating proved to be premature. Talbot spent eight months in gaol in Ireland, but at length he managed to get bail for £10,000. He pleaded ill-health, and a medical certificate, of dubious origin, allowed him to go to Paris, where he mysteriously returned to good health. Peter, his brother, was not so lucky, for he had genuine ill-health. Distemper did not save him from a cell in Dublin Castle, where he remained until his death two years later.

Talbot was now fifty-one and a widower. He married Frances Jennings, his first love, a widow of only thirty-three. In 1683 the Talbots obtained Ormonde's permission to return to Ireland, where Richard started to dabble in Irish politics. He called for changes in the three great monopolies of the Irish Protestants, the Privy Council, the judiciary, the magistracy and the army. At this point Charles II died, changing his whole life, and now his friend James II ascended the throne. James raised Talbot to the peerage as Baron Talbotstown, Viscount Baltinglass and Earl of Tyrconnel. He was promoted to Lieutenant General and was soon appointed Commander in Chief of the army in Ireland.

Tyrconnel was now earmarked to carry out James's great Catholic design in Ireland, which he had long sought to impress upon his brother Charles. Tyrconnel was now fifty-five, a man 'of stately presence'. Berwick recalled in his memoirs that he was "bold and resolute, of greater courage than conduct, naturally proud and passionate, of moderate parts but of an undoubted ambition". He was "a man of very good sense, very obliging but immoderately vain and full of cunning. He had not a military genius but much courage". Macaulay said that whenever he opened his mouth, he swore and cursed with great violence.

He was God's gift to wig-makers, for in heated moments he would throw his wig on the floor and stamp on it. In cases of great moment, he would hurl his wig into the fire. He would never let his true feelings be known to people, and it was not without cause that he became known as 'Lying Dick Talbot'. He was to become de facto dictator of Ireland.

James recalled the Lord Lieutenant, Ormonde, and this was the first step along the road to transforming the Irish army into a Catholic bulwark. Ormonde was riding to London in a coach when he read in a news sheet that the command of his own cavalry regiment had been given to 'Lying Dick'. James was not a month on the throne before Marcissus Luttrel was writing in his diary that the privy council was dissolved and a new one appointed. Two months later James made Monmouth's rebellion as an excuse to disarm the Irish militia, although the force had shown no signs of disloyalty throughout the Monmouth affair. The militia was exclusively Protestant, and its disbandment caused great alarm amongst the planters. Tyrconnel was now chosen for the more difficult task of transforming the Irish regular army from a Protestant force into a Catholic one.

Lord Clarendon was now appointed Lord Lieutenant of Ireland, and from the start Tyrconnel treated him with contempt. He made it clear that James, as a Roman Catholic, would want a Roman Catholic army. Tyrconnel furiously criticized the Acts of Settlement: "By God, my Lord, these Acts of Settlement and this New Interest are damned things!" He was fond of quarrelling with the Lord Lieutenant on the subject of sheriffs, for Clarendon had appointed none but Protestants, following the usual practices. "By God, my Lord, I must needs tell you that the sheriffs you made are generally rogues and Old Cromwellians", and "By God, for there has not been an honest man sheriff in Ireland these twenty years! By God, my Lord, you must not wonder if the Catholics do think you a little partial after your making such a lot of sheriffs". Tyrconnel, much to

Clarendon's relief, was planning a visit to London, on a mission which the Lord Lieutenant calculated would turn the Kingdom upside down. The planters shared the alarm of Clarendon when they heard that Tyrconnel was fulminating that the Reformation had ruined everything but that there were better times coming.

Tyrconnel made frequent visits to England, saying that it was for the sake of his health. He was plagued with gout, which probably accounts for his frequent outbursts, but he was also making sure of James's support in any altercation between himself and Clarendon. His wife, now a Lady of the Queen's Bedchamber, was playing a useful part. Tyrconnel now suggested that he should replace Clarendon as Lord Lieutenant, and Clarendon soon found that decisions regarding Ireland were being taken in London without any reference to himself. Sunderland, the Secretary of State, informed Clarendon that the civil and military administration was to be completely transformed, so that Catholics should have appointments. Clarendon was accused of being inexperienced and that James was in the hands of competent advisers on Irish matters in London.

Clarendon was being humiliated on all sides, and when he travelled through Ireland, the people treated him with contempt. The priests encouraged their flocks not to show him any respect. The peasants sang songs in praise of Tyrconnel. Clarendon noticed one day that one of his escorts was a Catholic, the work of Lying Dick. James wrote him letters, letting him know of his severe displeasure, and that Clarendon should do His Majesty's will with good grace. Clarendon's co-operation had been reluctant for he thoroughly disapproved of the policy which he had been called upon to administer. His brother, Rochester, fell from grace and with him fell Clarendon. He was recalled and replaced by Tyrconnel, who had to be content with the lesser title of Lord-Deputy, much to his displeasure. James felt that it would be unsafe to promote any Irishman however loyal to the office of Lord Lieutenant. There was in fact little difference between the two titles, for when there was no Lord Lieutenant, the Lord-Deputy reigned supreme.

Now by his ranting and ravings it seemed likely that Tyrconnel was ready to cut Protestant throats. He had already nearly completed the task of transforming the Protestant Irish army into a Catholic one. Officers were deprived of commissions without being given a penny in compensation. The rank and file received similar treatment. Four or five hundred men were dismissed from one regiment on the grounds that they were below regulation height, although it was obvious that they were taller than the Irish replacements. The Lord-Deputy's supporters were claiming that by Christmas 1686 there would not be an Englishman left in the whole army.

The size of Tyrconnel's new Irish army alarmed Protestants, for where Ormonde had been content with eight regiments, Tyrconnel had six times that number. These men were fierce and undisciplined and ill-armed, men who never passed an Englishman without a curse and who were a terror to Protestant innkeepers, eating and drinking everything and paying for nothing, for they were hardly ever paid. Basically the army was made up of good material; what it needed was good officers to train them, but here Tyrconnel's policy fell down, for the commissions were granted on grounds of religion. Macaulay says that ". . . Commissions were scattered profusely among idle cosherers who claimed to be descended from good Irish families, yet even thus the supply of captains and lieutenants fell short of the demand, and many companies were commanded by cobblers, tailors and footmen". Macaulay's evidence is borne out by D'Avaux, who arrived in Ireland as French ambassador in 1688.

Tyrconnel now started to reshape the civil administration, starting with the sheriffs; new sheriffs being appointed throughout Ireland. They were Catholic to a man, except in Donegal, where a Protestant was picked instead of a Catholic by mistake. The Protestants were further alarmed; some of these sheriffs having been burnt in the arm for theft. The larger towns, which had Protestant corporations since the time of Cromwell had their charters revoked; new corporations were appointed in which Catholics were included. This early attempt at power sharing went smoothly, except at Londonderry, where James wrote that they were 'a stubborn people'. Tyrconnel replaced the Lord Chancellor, the Chief Justice of the King's Bench, the Chief Baron of the Exchequer, the Attorney General and a number of puisne judges with Catholics, who had little qualification for the jobs. The new Chief Justice of the King's Bench was Thomas Nugent, a troublesome and impertinent man. Many were clever enough lawyers, and the best of them, Stephen Rice, said that he would drive a coach and horses through the Acts of Settlement. Stephen Rice was appointed Chief Baron of the Irish Exchequer Court, and it was here that the Irish flocked with their writs of ejectment and trespass against the Protestants. A Jacobite wrote that Tyrconnel's policies were making more enemies for James than all the other mistakes of his administration. These mistakes were not apparent at the time, and many southern Protestants decided to go while the going was good. Protestant army officers made for Holland to offer their swords to William of Orange. Merchants sold off their stock and headed for England, sailing across the Irish Sea in open boats, choosing to trust the weather rather than the Catholics. The refugees brought hair-raising stories with them to England. But it would not be long before the king would apply to England the policies he had so far followed in Ireland.

The government assured people that James's administration in Ireland was liberal. People were assured that Irish Protestants lived in freedom, peace and security. Government agents soon spread the word through the taverns and coffee houses of England that Irish Protestants were living happily under Tyrconnel, but the English preferred to believe the accounts given by the refugees. Many southern Protestants were unable to leave, and they expected to be robbed first and then murdered. Increasingly eyes were turned on Derry, where as we have seen, the Apprentice Boys had closed the gates upon a Catholic army.

Chapter 8

The Flight to Londonderry

Tyrconnel had at last made up his mind to support James, and he now issued what amounted to be a 'levee en masse'. It met with an enthusiastic response and a banner in Dublin Castle was embroidered with the words "Now or Never! Now and Forever!" Anyone who was able to raise the required number of troops, received an officer's commission. Within two months, these methods are said to have raised 100,000 men, but only about half of these could be classed as soldiers. According to Macaulay, the rest were bandits. The troops behaved in an irresponsible manner, for their officers could not pay them, and the latter could barely support themselves. They lived off the land — in other words off the Protestants, who had now been disarmed for the second time. The Protestants were ordered to hand in all swords and firelocks, and were warned that anyone found in possession of arms after a given date, would have their house looted. Even those who obeyed Tyrconnel did not escape plundering.

There was a Captain Barton, who had been given an official protection for his house at Carrickmacross, County Monaghan, which he had left under care of his servants whilst he was in Dublin. A troop of MacMahon's cavalry produced the protection note. The troop commander said that he only wished to billet some of his men in the house so that it might be better held for the king and Captain Barton. No sooner were the troops admitted than they started to plunder, and within hours they had caused £10,000 worth of damage. Captain Barton protested, but it only got him into more trouble, for his house was burnt to the ground.

In West Cork, it is said that Protestants were robbed of their furniture and cattle in broad daylight. The troops, with pipers playing before them, robbed Protestants left right and centre. Chief Justice Nugent said at the Cork Assizes that the robberies were necessary evils and it was evident that he had no intention of trying to stop them. The judges had set out upon their Spring circuit a month earlier than usual that year, with the intention of punishing Catholics found victimizing Protestants, but it soon became clear that it was their intention of punishing Protestants who had dared to take up arms in defence of their property. Livestock was targeted by the Catholics, and the troops feasted on Protestant mutton. Stories of the gluttony of the Irish soon circulated amongst the planters. There were stories of animals being boiled alive. With the coming of Lent, the

Catholics refrained from eating meat, but not from killing livestock. Cows would be killed for the sake of obtaining a pair of brogues from the hide. Sheep were slaughtered in thousands for their fleeces, their carcases left in the fields to decompose and poison the air. Avaux in a report to Louis XIV estimated that in six weeks 50,000 cattle had been slaughtered in the above fashion, and the number of sheep killed he estimated at 300,000. It would take Ireland ten years to recover from the damage that had been caused in a few weeks.

Ulster remained free from these outrages. When the province heard about Tyrconnel's plans, they began to enlist their tenants into regiments, which were armed with whatever weapons happened to be available. Protestant gentry marched about Ulster inducing the people to arm, and the whole province did this, except the towns of Carrickfergus and Armagh, which were still dominated by Tyrconnel's garrisons.

In the early days of January 1689, the Protestant gentry had a lot to lose if Tyrconnel's policies were successful. The Earl Mount-Alexander was chosen to head all the Protestant forces raised in Down, Antrim, Armagh and Monaghan; his qualifications for this high command are obscure. In mid-January these four counties formed a Council of the North at Hillsborough, a few miles south-east of Belfast, and they at once struck up a correspondence with other Protestants in the North. They wrote to the ex-Viceroy, Clarendon, asking him to induce William to send over troops quickly, together with arms, ammunition and money which would be required to save Ireland for the Crown. They estimated that 10,000 foot and 1,500 horse would be essential and in addition 20,000 muskets and ammunition for local volunteers, with commissions for their officers. These requests, in a letter, were taken to England by Captain Baldwin Leighton, who was considered to be loyal.

Leighton was a captain in Sir Thomas Newcomen's regiment, another which escaped Tyrconnel's purge. Leighton had persuaded four other officers, Lieutenants Hamilton, Tubman and Barry, and Ensign Talbot, to resign their commissions and support the Protestant cause. These officers in turn had persuaded a hundred and fifty Protestant other ranks of the regiment to do the same. Several other of Newcomen's officers deserted. Very little use was made of these additions to the Protestant interest, and despite lavish preparations, the work of the Council of the North was lethargic. They swung from gloom at the Council's foundation to ecstasy, and they were now convinced that there would be no war in Ireland, a belief which was strengthened when they heard that William and Mary had become the English sovereigns. The Council had the proclamation published in all towns in Ulster under their control. They were certain that Tyrconnel must now come to terms with William or that help in great strength would arrive from England. The Council therefore made no elaborate war preparations and contented themselves with mustering a few companies which were scattered in a number of garrison points.

The Council launched a half-hearted attack upon Tyrconnel's garrison at Carrickfergus. The skirmish petered out and both sides agreed that an account

41

of the affair should be taken to the Lord-Deputy at Dublin by a friar named O'Haggerty. The friar was able to report to Tyrconnel that the Protestants were ill-prepared for war. They were untrained, and had few experienced officers, and were mostly without arms. Those that had weapons were not in a fit state for use. The numbers of Protestants were small. Tyrconnel still hoped that the Ulster Protestants would surrender without a fight and he had made no serious attempt to reassert James's authority in the North. On 7th March, he issued a free pardon to all those who would lay down their arms and submit, but if they failed to do this, they would be treated as traitors to His Majesty. He assured the Protestants that the innocent would not suffer with the guilty. But there could be no hope of pardon for men like the Earl Mount-Alexander, Lord Kingston, Lord Masserene and his son, Robert Colville, Arthur Rawdon, John Magill, John Hawkins, Robert Sanderson and Francis Hamilton.

Tyrconnel had no intention of making peace with William, and he eagerly awaited James's arrival in Ireland with French backing. He acted with an energy which far outmatched that of the Ulster Protestants. All Ireland, except Ulster, had been mobilized for James's cause. People had been asked to contribute cash, malt, beef, cheese, butter, herrings, leather, stockings, wool, cloth and linen. Plate, money and arms had been confiscated from Protestant houses and their horses impounded for the service of King James. Tyrconnel was able to raise a force of 7,000 men, one-third of them regulars, with five pieces of artillery. Richard Hamilton was promoted to the rank of Lieutenant General and given command of the army, even though he had ratted to William and was now re-ratting to James. His task was to bring Ulster back to allegiance to the king.

Hamilton marched north without delay. Close behind him came a Presbyterian clergyman called Alexander Osborne, who had once held a living in Tyrone but was now a minister in Dublin. His task was to bring to the Protestants Tyrconnel's terms, which in effect were those of 7th March 1689. On 9th March he passed Hamilton's army on its way north. He found the Hillsborough Council in session at Loughbrickland and explained to them that the Lord-Deputy was willing to grant a free pardon in return for handing over all arms and serviceable horses. The alternative to this was to be crushed by Hamilton's army, which marched on Belfast, Coleraine and Londonderry. The Lord-Deputy said that men, women and boys now armed with half-pikes and baggonets in counties Cavan, Monaghan, Tyrone and Londonderry would massacre the British if his terms were not agreed upon.

George Walker was still in his County Tyrone rectory and was said to have a certain Episcopalian prejudice, and in his account of the siege, accused Osborne of being in Tyrconnel's pay as a spy upon the whole North. On the contrary Osborne was proving to be quite a useful intelligence officer for the Protestants, for he was able to inform them that "the Irish army, though their horses were good, yet their riders were but contemptible fellows, many of them having been lately cowherds, etc.". The Irish, he informed them, were short of ammunition. He told them that it would be fatal to accept Tyrconnel's terms, for the Lord-Deputy would break faith with them, just as he had done with the Protestants of the South. They would be reduced to "poverty and slavery".

Osborne was invited to appear before the Council in person, when he told them to get ready to defend their lives and not put faith in Tyrconnel. They were "to defend themselves to the utmost". The Council was ready to follow his advice, for Captain Baldwin Leighton had just returned from England, bringing Lord Mount-Alexander a letter from William. The king expressed his approval of the measures Protestants were taking and promised them that he would take all measures to relieve the pressures they were under. The Council sent Tyrconnel a firm reply to his terms, saying that they would be horrified by the shedding of blood, but that they would not lay down their arms. They would agree to treat with the Lord-Deputy, but only in terms consistent with the safety of their religion, their lives and liberties.

Meanwhile Hamilton was making a speedy northern advance, and although Osborne had given them accurate information, they were surprised when they heard that the army was almost upon them. Arthur Rawdon, a bold soldier, earning him the title of 'Cock of the North', sent out a small body of cavalry to confront Hamilton at the village of Dromore. The Protestants were humiliated, for when the Irish army was in sight, the Protestants fled. They were chased through the streets of Hillsborough and beyond, and lost almost a hundred men. Many now made for the relative safety of their homes, where they accepted "protections" from Hamilton.

News of the 'Break of Dromore' reached Belfast, then a village of a few hundred on the mud flats of the Lagan. People left Belfast for Stranraer, for word came that the Irish army was slaughtering all before it, sparing neither age nor sex. Stranraer was packed with refugees, so that people were huddled together on the beach and taking shelter from the rain under upturned boats. Most believed that the Protestant cause was lost and took ship for Scotland or England. The Earl Mount-Alexander disappeared from the pages of history. He took passage from Donaghadee for England, with the excuse that he was one of the unpardonables.

There were still some 4.000 Protestants that had survived the 'Break of Dromore'. The 'Cock of the North' collected his troops and retreated towards Coleraine, and along with him came a multitude of civilians, who had no intention of having their throats cut by the Irish. The Protestants fled from the southern part of the province; some to Coleraine, some to Londonderry, and some to Enniskillen. Macaulay wrote that the fugitives broke down the bridges and burned the ferryboats. Whole towns were left without one inhabitant. The people of Omagh destroyed their town so perfectly that there was not a roof left to shelter the enemy. The people of Cavan migrated en masse to Enniskillen; the roads were deep in mire, and people ploughed through the mud up to their knees.

On 15th March the 'Cock of the North' reached Coleraine; a town whose ramshackle defences had been its salvation nearly fifty years before. If Coleraine fell, only Londonderry and Enniskillen would be left. Hamilton's Catholic army however wasted a lot of time looting Lisburn, Antrim and Masserene Castle. This gave Major Gustavus Hamilton an extra twelve days from the time of the Cock's arrival to organize defences. There was a mud wall and a deep ditch protecting three sides of Coleraine and the River Bann, over which was a wooden bridge, guarding the fourth side.

Richard Hamilton's army arrived on 27th March and informed the garrison that they would pay them a visit next day about ten o'clock. Protestants and Catholics bombarded each other with cannon, and the Irish army started to work its way through the hedges and gardens that lay outside the town. An inconclusive duel of musketry and artillery continued until dusk. It began to snow heavily and the Irish withdrew under cover of the storm. It is believed that they lost about sixty men, but the exact number was uncertain for the Catholics had no time to bury their dead and had piled the corpses into a house, burning them to ashes. They had many wounded, and they were so demoralized by the sight of a body of horse and foot drawn up under Lord Blayney on a hill outside Coleraine, that they fled in panic, abandoning two guns and much baggage, which they recovered next day. Richard Hamilton had been so confident that the Protestants would surrender that he brought with him provisions for only two days, whilst the Protestants with only three men killed, were heartened.

But Hamilton knew that reinforcements were on their way; six regiments of foot and two of horse, which were assembling at Charlemont, so he was undismayed at the setback. Hamilton decided to press on towards Londonderry, reasoning that rather than be cut off from Derry, the Coleraine garrison would abandon the town. The Catholic troops fanned out from Coleraine along the east side of the Bann, looking for a place to cross, whilst the garrison replied by destroying the bridge at Portglenone, twenty miles upstream, and posting men at key places on the Londonderry side of the river, at Toome, Newferry, Magherafelt, Moneymore, Portglenone, Kilrea and Agivey.

Coleraine was held by 3,000 men under command of Sir Tristram Bereford, who sent two regiments of infantry and a few troops to march and countermarch, while they watched the Catholics do the same on the opposite shore. All the time the Protestants were looking for a weak spot where they could cross. The Protestants however were thin on the ground, and they could not hold the river line for long, and on 4th April, the Williamites were driven in at Moneymore by the Catholics from Charlemont. On 7th April, Hamilton's men were across the Bann, for they had found some boats at Portglenone which had been carelessly abandoned. Bad weather played havoc with both sides; March had been wet, cold and stormy and in the following weeks was so bad that the rivers burst their banks and fevers and dysentery prevailed everywhere. Colonel Edmonstone, who commanded the Protestants at Portglenone, caught a chill from which he died. Sir Arthur Rawdon — who had been in command at Moneymore and a physically weak man — never really recovered from the weather and had to be invalided back to England before the siege began.

Gustavus Hamilton of Coleraine, reacted just as the Irish expected him. He headed for Londonderry before his lines of communication were cut. He was accompanied by droves of countryfolk who carried their belongings along with them. He called in his outlying detachments from along the Bann and destroyed the bridge. All the country came towards Londonderry as a last resort — from not only Coleraine, but from Antrim, Down, Armagh, Monaghan, Tyrone and Donegal. The Coleraine garrison was later criticized for their inability to hold Coleraine, and it was said that there was not enough good officers. It was said that the rabble panicked and many good horses and arms, as well as the riches of the town, fell into Catholic hands. However George Walker praised the men of Coleraine, for "certainly there could not be better men in the world".

Even in the flight to Derry there seemed to be little salvation. It would take Richard Hamilton's force only a few days to reach the city, whilst Irish forces were marching north-west from Charlemont by way of Omagh and Strabane. Another Jacobite army was marching north from Dublin, plundering and looting in their path, as they moved at incredible speed. They were led by a strong French military mission of experienced officers, and were accompanied by James II himself. James had set foot on Ireland for the first time, and he now wanted to persuade the Protestants to surrender Londonderry, so that he could cross to Scotland to recover his lost kingdom.

News from Ulster was pessimistic, for the number of Protestants in the north of Ireland was estimated at 100,000, many whom had fled. They were ill-armed and had no money, and were thronged into the area around Londonderry, where outside the walls there was little safety and within them room for only about 3,000. The only hope for Londonderry, it seemed, lay in its Governor, Lieutenant Colonel Robert Lundy; it was hoped that Londonderry could hold out for some time.

Chapter 9

"If Stones Could Speak . . ."

Back at the beginning of the century, the Lord-Deputy, Sir Arthur Chichester, saw that things were going wrong for the Ulster plantation. Too many lands had been reserved for Irish grantees and far too many had been given to undertakers from Great Britain, who were men of little resources, to whom it was more profitable to keep on the Irish as tenants than import British colonists. It undermined the principle that Irish tenants should be confined to the estates of Irish grantees, servitors and the Church. The Catholics wanted to do anything to remain on the lands of their fathers, and went to all lengths to please the British, while privately wanting to rebel. The undertakers were willing to take the risk of rebellion for the sake of profit. Chichester was convinced that such an attitude on behalf of the British must sooner or later provoke an uprising. The Irish were regarded as 'Gibeonites, hewers of wood and drawers of water'. Chichester was however resolved to make the plantation as effective as possible, despite its shortcomings.

The region of Derry and Coleraine had great natural resources, but the undertakers had shown little enthusiasm, for warlike clans like the O'Cahans were still on the prowl. Only Coleraine was thriving, and this was thanks to the energy of Sir Thomas Phillips, a Welsh soldier of fortune. Phillips had served against Hugh O'Neill, and as one of the leading servitors, he had decided to remain in Ulster; he made great efforts to foster a colony at Coleraine. He fortified the town, he built thirty small thatched houses, he set up a water mill and spent money on developing a market. Ships from Scotland sailed up the Bann with their goods and carried back timber and agricultural products. He spent all his money on the project and often risked his life.

Spring 1609, saw Phillips in London and this came to the ear of the king's chief minister, Robert Cecil, now Lord Salisbury. Phillips was in London to claim some lands near Coleraine and he wanted the powerful London Company to act as a collective undertaker for the County of Coleraine and its neighbouring districts. Salisbury agreed that the Company was the best means to undertake the colonization of the county. When the Company seemed later to be falling down in its commission, Phillips became London's enemy. He had the City dragged before the Court of Star Chamber. It was fined huge sums and its charter revoked. However in the beginning he was an enthusiastic supporter of

Salisbury's plans. It seemed that he would have to hand over his own little colony at Coleraine, but for that he received compensation. He estimated that the City's original investment would have to be £50,000, of which over half would be needed for the works at Derry and Coleraine. A further £8,620 would be needed to stock the country with cattle and crops, to arrange transport, to pay workmen, factors and experts to build forts, storehouses and bridges. Another £12,000 would be needed to establish profit-making ventures as the breeding of pigs in the woods, setting up timber mills, tanneries, linen manufactories and shipyards. An export trade in timber, beef, hides, tallow, oatmeal, yarn and fish had to be established. An investment of £2,800 in cattle and tillage, he estimated, would yield a profit of £1,000 in the first year.

Phillips wrote a paper outlining his proposals. He said that the best places to start would be Coleraine and the ruined town of Derry, and that they could be made almost impregnable by land. A flourishing export trade could be set up between these towns and England, Scotland, Spain and the Straits of Gibraltar, and even Newfoundland. The natural resources of the Bann and Foyle valleys would yield a rich harvest, and would relieve unemployment in England with the introduction of settlers. It would also relieve disease in the overcrowded capital. The city's merchants could find a market for their goods throughout Ulster, and London would do considerably better than a previous effort made by Bristol in Dublin five hundred years before.

The government now tried to sound out a few wealthy individuals, starting with the Lord Mayor, Sir Humphrey Welf, who was persuaded by Salisbury to meet Sir Thomas Phillips. Sir John Jolles of the Draper's Company and William Cockayne of the Skinners, accompanied the Lord Mayor to the meeting. Both had had experience in the Tyrone wars as victualling contractors to the English army and therefore had some knowledge of Ulster. Cockayne became so involved in the export of Bushmills whiskey that he became addicted to it. The City fathers wanted to know as soon as possible what return they would have on their investment. Phillips was sure that he had satisfied them on all points, and said that if his advice were followed, returns in the first year would be in excess of £9,000. The City seemed happy with the arrangements, and all the liveries were called upon to submit lists of contributors, listing the individual amounts promised as well as the names of those who refused to subscribe. The livery men however were not enthusiastic, for they realized that the nature of the country would make colonization difficult, expensive and dangerous. The historian of the Irish Society wrote that the livery companies "had little stomach for the project; left to themselves, without pressure from the Court of Aldermen and the heavy threat of the king's displeasure, they would have dismissed it out of hand".

The Fishmongers were reluctant as well, and only seven of the forty-six members of the Grocers, the Lord Mayor's own company, were willing to risk their own money. The Skinners saw that there might be profits to be made, but they used the excuse that a legal limitation on the spending of their own funds, made it impossible for them to undergo the plantation. Twenty-five of them, however, were willing to make investments as individuals: The Master, William Cockayne headed the list with £250. A humble £1 was promised by the Barber-Surgeons. Two small companies, the Bowyers and the Fletchers were excused altogether by the Court of Aldermen on grounds that they were very poor men and that their trades were not in good condition.

There was enough support to justify taking matters further and four citizens were employed to go to Derry and Coleraine to make maps and judge for themselves the fitness of the areas for plantation. John Rowley and John Munn of the Grocers — John Broad the Goldsmith and Robert Treswell the Painter-Stainer, headed for Ulster with £300 from the City Chamberlain, Thomas Phillips accompanying them as a guide. Chichester had been advised about the mission, and he was instructed by the Privy Council to give the Londoners every assistance. A private note stated that the viewers received only the best impressions. The guides were to be discreet persons who would lead the Londoners only by the most attractive routes and lodge them in English houses. They were to point out the advantages of colonizing O'Cahan's country. The chief guide was Thomas Phillips, who took the party first to Coleraine and then over the hills to Limavady where the Lord-Deputy welcomed them, saying that if the Londoners went ahead with their plantation, then the whole of Ireland would be assured for the English Crown.

They left one of their members behind at Limavady, for he had been taken ill, and he was persuaded not to return to England lest the Society used this as an excuse not to invest money. The remaining three went to Lifford and Derry and then returned to Coleraine by a different road. They went south to the Loughinsolin Woods, and then to Lough Neagh, where at Toome, a smith produced steel within an hour from local ore, which had the approval of John Broad, the goldsmith. They then sailed back down the Bann to Coleraine. They were not shown the desolated Sperrin Mountains, but were shepherded down the fertile valley of the Foyle, the Bann, the Roe and the Faughan.

Treswell, the Painter-Stainer, wrote to Salisbury that they were very impressed with what they had seen, and that the plantation would be successful. Samples of Ulster products were bought at bargain prices and shipped to London, so that the Lord Mayor would be impressed with the colonization idea. Phillips was so sure that the plantation would go ahead, that he ordered 10,000 trees to be felled and seasoned, so that they would be ready for the following Spring.

Articles of Agreement were signed between the Crown and the City, which meant that the Londoner's concessions were accepted. Derry and Coleraine were to be granted municipal privileges similar to those enjoyed by London, Dublin and the Cinque Ports. The king agreed to maintain a force in the area sufficient for the planters' safety. In return the City had to build sixty houses at Derry and forty at Coleraine by 1st November 1610, together with fortifications. The remaining houses and fortifications had to be completed within a further twelve months.

To manage its plantations in Ulster, a new company was set up. It had a governor, William Cockayne, a deputy governor and twenty-four assistants. It was formed along the lines of other companies that were taking shape at this time to colonize distant lands, amongst them the Virginia and East India Companies. The full title of the company was 'The Society of the New Plantation in Ulster within the realm of Ireland'. This was shortened to become known as 'The Honourable the Irish Society'.

John Rowley, one of the viewers, became the Society's chief resident agent in Ulster; he had a chief assistant who had immediate responsibility for Coleraine. However a number of livery men in London defaulted on their promised contribution, and they were imprisoned by the Lord Mayor. Despite the good reports, there was little enthusiasm in London. Land was promised at four pence an acre, but there were few takers. There was no guarantee that the Irish would not rebel and that the planters would not be massacred.

Despatched from London to the new estates were 130 masons, carpenters and other craftsmen. The Lord-Deputy was asked that they could obtain food at normal prices and to enlist a local labour force for the task of felling trees and for other rough work. Reports however soon came back that most of the London craftsmen were unsuitable. The assurance that they would find in Ulster everything they needed turned out to be untrue, and some downed tools whilst others demanded higher wages. There was no money at Derry to meet the demands, and activities ceased, and only the arrival of Rowley and Beresford at Coleraine with £400 in cash, allowed work at the town to go ahead.

Chichester, visiting Coleraine in August 1610, was surprised at the progress that had been made. John Davies, who accompanied him, was enthusiastic about the plans. They found a great store of timber at Coleraine together with other materials, and they were sure that God would bless the plantation. The timber had been felled from the woods at Glenconkeyne and brought in boats down the Bann. Coleraine was taking on an hexagonal shape, with one side protected by the River Bann, and the other five by an earth rampart and a ditch. Behind these 'walls' tenements were built out of the timber, fitted with chimneys and roofed with slate. The largest of these tenements measured eighteen feet by twenty-three feet, with three storeys and six rooms. The rent was £5 a year. The old church was repaired and a malt house built with a brew house, a smithy, a water mill and a cattle pound. Down by the Bann, a landing stage was built for a ferry, and soon there would be a bridge. A quay sixty feet long was built for ships and barges. Further upstream, a dock led to a shipyard and a shipwright's house. The Gaels must have wondered at the enterprise of the planters.

At Derry, a new fortified town was planned, much larger than the earlier settlement of Docwra's. Landing places were made at each side of the Foyle for a cross-river ferry, and a quay was constructed. There was a ready supply of stone and slate, with wood and coal for burning lime. The houses were all to be stone built, with window frames and doorframes of timber, built to an already planned design. The rents were to be similar to Coleraine.

49

D

Midway between Derry and Coleraine, another little plantation town was taking shape at Limavady, called Newtownlimavady to distinguish it from the old O'Cahan fort of the same name about a mile further up the River Roe. Limavady fell outside the plantation's jurisdiction, for here Sir Thomas Phillips had received a grant of 3,000 acres in compensation for having surrendered his estates at Coleraine to the Irish Society. Phillips laid out streets and built a water mill, together with a two-storied inn, to serve people travelling between Derry and Coleraine. Timber was supplied from Glenconkeyne, and there was plenty of stone at Limavady; from the shores of Lough Neagh he could obtain shells for making lime.

By January 1611, the Irish Society's plans were under way. Settlers from London were beginning to arrive. However the English workmen were causing trouble and John Rowley was told to stop their pay, to discharge the idle persons, and if necessary to send them back to London. There were excessive drinking facilities and Rowley was instructed to restrain hard drinkers. From now on there should be only two or three taverns and two alehouses at Coleraine, and four taverns and not more than ten alehouses at Derry.

Coleraine and Derry received their charters in 1613, when Derry was renamed Londonderry to symbolize its links with London. It became the new county town of the newly-created county of Londonderry, which absorbed the old county of Coleraine. The new county was almost twice the size of the old, taking in parts of Donegal, Antrim and Tyrone. Coleraine and Derry were the direct responsibility of the City of London, working through the Irish Society. The twelve great London livery companies, many of which had smaller liveries associated with them, managed the rest of the county, with the exception of church lands and grantees like Phillips.

Some little towns in the county today recall the founding livery company's duties, such as Drapestown and Salterstown. The Skinners were settled in the Dungiven region. There were also the Goldsmiths, Grocers, Fishmongers, Merchant Taylors, Haberdashers, Clothworkers, Vintners, Ironmongers and Mercers.

The little plantation towns were often built with long, straight, very wide streets. One town, Moneymore, enjoyed piped water, but this did not stop the citizens from complaining that the supply was inadequate and that the streets were foul with mud, so much so that men had to wear high boots to get from one house to another. The Drapers' agent, Robert Russell, diverted most of the water into a brewing enterprise of his own and was said to have bought houses to convert them into pubs. It was said that he was paying workmen partly in beer, with the result that there was much brawling in the muddy streets. A commission of enquiry, sent over in 1613, found that Rowley and Beresford had lined their own pockets at the City's expense, so there were sinners in high places as well. Neither were able to resist the temptation for going for a quick profit. They had despoiled the woods of Loughinsolin by taking the timber for pipe staves and barrel staves instead of allowing it to grow. Rowley ignored the

Society's warning that this was contrary to the Articles of Agreement. The chief offender was Rowley's own tenant, Oliver Nugent. When Thomas Phillips tried to stop this plundering of the forests, he got no thanks, but instead received a rude letter from the Deputy Governor of the Society, ordering him to stop meddling. This turned Phillips into an enemy of the Society, which was to cost it dear.

The natives were invaluable to the British undertakers, for they produced food, paid rent and laboured. It was part of the original plan to remove all the natives from chosen areas, but the Society was allowing them to stay on. Chichester complained that the Society's agents were persuading many Irishmen to stay who would not have moved. They were bringing Irishmen from Tyrone into Loughinsolin, where the natives were now more numerous than they had ever been. Chichester observed that the people of Coleraine county, who had up till now treated judges of assize and other public figures with respect, had behaved in an offhand manner at the last circuit, which was attributed to the insolence of the agents. They had not hesitated to interfere with the authority of Thomas Phillips, to whom Chichester had entrusted the general supervision of the area.

The Irish were caught between two stools, between their wanting to stay and their fear of being removed. They wanted to arm themselves, and their priests were encouraging them, telling them that the king would not protect them and that they were regarded as a vagabond people by the British. Chichester thought that a revolt was likely. Later he was to write to Cockayne that he had always been willing to give the Society all the help it needed, but that his advice was not followed. He pointed out that it was essential to fill Coleraine and Derry with British settlers and in the rest of the City's lands. He had already warned the Society that the work of plantation would be opposed by the natives, who were many in number. Nevertheless he said that he was confident in the planters, but that there were others of questionable character.

Early in 1613, Sir Arthur Chichester was created Lord Chichester, Baron of Belfast. Towards the end of 1614, he was recalled as Lord-Deputy of Ireland, but there is no reason to suppose that his recall was due to his refusal to persecute Catholics in the country. James however assured him that he had served well in Ireland, and presently he returned there as Lord Treasurer, but he no longer directly influenced affairs in Ulster.

Sometimes the Irish Society made efforts to mend its ways, for in 1616 it called upon each of the great livery companies to send one or two craftsmen, with their families, to Ulster to set up in business. They were to be respectable people and not layabouts or drunkards. The Irish Society proposed to send over twelve boys from Christ's Hospital, with other poor fellows, to serve as apprentices and servants. The Bluecoat boys arrived at Coleraine and Londonderry, but their fate is unknown, nor has their school anything to say about these youngsters.

Nicholas Pinnar had made a detailed inspection of Ulster in 1618, and it was apparent that the plantation was under way. Pinnar found that 107 castles with bawns had been built in the six escheated counties, together with nineteen castles without bawns and forty-two bawns without castles, as well as nearly 1,900 'English houses'; this was despite gloomy reports four years earlier by Sir Josias Bodley, director general and overseer of Irish fortifications. Pinnar reckoned that in the six escheated counties there were now 1,974 families together with cottages. A military force of 6,000 English and Scots might be mustered. If one were to add the Lowland Protestant Scots who had joined Randall MacDonnell in North Antrim and the 2,000 able Scotsmen in the Hamilton and Montgomery settlements in Clandeboye, the fighting strength of the Protestants might be as much as 12,000. However the English tenants in their anxiety about the future, were doing no ploughing. The Irish who were allowed to remain on the land, did no ploughing either, for they never knew when they might be evicted. The Scots however vigorously tilled the land, and if it had not been for them there would have been few crops in those years. Every parish was to produce its posse of vigilantes, for the counties were full of wood-kern, who committed outrages. In the Winter of 1616, these vigilantes managed to kill over forty of these outlaws. Revelyn O'Neill, a rebel leader, was captured by his fellow countrymen and handed over to the English. He was hanged outside Garvagh and his head displayed upon the walls of Coleraine. In the 1641 rebellion, his ghost witnessed revenge at what was for ever after known as Revelyn's Hill. The wood-kerns could always be kept in check by stern measures, but Pinnar warned that the settlers, especially in County Derry would be exterminated if there were a general uprising. The castles, 126 altogether, with or without bawns, would have to be the lines of defence.

If the English or Scots were overrun there would be no alternative but to fall back behind the walls of Coleraine and Derry. At Derry, fortifications were going ahead and by 1622, 240 stone houses had been built together with a town hall, a new palace for the bishop and a free school. Derry was surrounded by a strong stone wall with four gates, all of which had been fortified. There was a new cathedral, Saint Columb's, in which a mural tablet still tells about the building:–

If stones could speak
Then London's praise
Should sound who
Built this Church and City
From the Ground.

The walls of Derry were all of good lime and stone, with a dry ditch outside for more than half the circuit, eight feet deep and thirty across. However greater effort was needed, and the City of London was directed to build guardhouses, sentinel houses, stairs and passages to the bulwarks and ramparts where they were deficient. Along the walls stood the cannons, many of them old even then, and one dated back to 1590 with the initials 'ER' on it. Another was inscribed with the arms of the Irish Society, and others were presented by the London

Companies. There was 'Roaring Meg', so called because of the intensity of the sound, a gift from the Fishmongers in 1642. It was eleven feet long and four a half feet wide at the thickest part. In a postscript in 1628, the Commissioners warned that Derry was not a natural place of defence and lay open to attack from the sea and by land; it would not be 'tenable if any foreign enemy were to come before it'. The city was overlooked by high ground across the Foyle, but the walls had never been made to withstand siege by professional forces, but were built to withstand an onrush by Irish peasantry.

Chapter 10

Governor Lundy

King James II landed at Kinsale in 1689, two days before the Protestants were routed at Dromore. He had spent the previous three months seeking French help for the recovery of his throne. Louis XIV had treated James with respect, but he made it plain that he would only act in the interests of France. If James could help stop Europe from the tendency to unite in the face of French domination, that would be okay. If James hated William of Orange, he planned to recover his throne with Louis's blessing, so French assistance would be forthcoming. An Irishman called Roth and a French naval officer, the Marquis de Pointis, were sent to Ireland to assess the situation. They reported to Louis that a diversion in Ireland was a good idea, and that James's plans to lead his cause with French money and arms was also sound.

Louis was reluctant to commit France to an Irish war, for James, who had so easily given up his throne, might show the same weakness in its recovery. Later when Louis agreed to send some French regiments to Ireland, it was on condition that James should provide an equal number of troops for France to serve on the Continent. Four hundred captains, lieutenants, cadets, gunners, and generals, were selected to organize and train the Irish army. Muskets were also provided for twenty regiments, and money was forthcoming to the tune of 500,000 gold crowns. The able French diplomat, the Comte d'Avaux, accompanied the expedition as ambassador to King James, perhaps the future King of England. There were English and Scottish Jacobites in the Irish army, who had loyally followed James into exile. James's two illegitimate sons also accompanied him; he had fathered them by Marlborough's sister, Arabella Churchill. The eldest, the nineteen-year-old Duke of Berwick, was loyal and was soon to show himself a good soldier. However, Henry known as the Grand Prior, because of a sinecure, bestowed upon him from infancy by James, was quarrelsome. According to Avaux he got so drunk every day after his arrival in Ireland that he could not mount a horse all that summer.

Louis was kind to James up until the latter's departure for Ireland. He gave him his own cuirass. Cabin furniture, camp furniture, tents, bedding, plate were superb. Louis said upon James's departure that he hoped he would never see him again, hinting that it was best for James to regain his kingdom. If James had to return he would also find in Louis an agreeable host. The French courtiers were also hoping that they might never see James again. They had regarded him with contempt, for they had to listen over and over again to the story of his downfall. James could not see that he might have been responsible for the change of kings in England. They said that if anyone knew why James was at Louis's court, then it was only necessary for people to listen to him. The more they saw of James, the less they pitied him for the loss of his kingdom. Ireland, they thought, was the best place for him and he could act as if he had never heard of the Prince of Orange.

Avaux also was already beginning to have his doubts about James. As the expedition was assembling at Brest, he heard James talk about top secret matters within earshot of the crew. Avaux also said that the chief difficulty was the irresolution of the king, who often changed his mind, and then found it hard to decide for the best.

At length, the expedition arrived at Kinsale. James moved inland to Cork where Lord-Deputy Tyrconnel had come to meet him. James made Tyrconnel a duke; he had brought the king some good news. In the three southern provinces, the Protestants had been disarmed and were terrified. James therefore had nothing to fear, and Richard Hamilton should have little trouble in crushing the North. The resistance at Enniskillen was trifling, and Tyrconnel assured his king that the opposition at Londonderry could be dealt with.

James set out on the slow journey from Kinsale to Dublin, and Avaux observed that from Kilkenny onwards the country was deserted. It should have been full of crops and people, but nevertheless the progress had a triumphant air. Outlaws lined the roads, armed with skeans and half-pikes. Pipers played in front and frieze mantles were spread Raleigh-fashion in front of the king. Villagers danced excitedly in the streets. Dublin had a population of only 30,000, but it was now the second largest city in the British Isles. It gave James a great welcome; James entering the city on horseback so that the people could see him. The streets were strewn with greenery and flowers, and there was a heavy military presence. Forty girls dressed in white and carrying bouquets stood in strategic points to welcome the king. The Duke of Tyrconnel bore the sword of state before his master; the judges, heralds, Lord Mayor and aldermen formed a procession. A Te Deum was sung in thanksgiving and the pipers and harpers played 'The King shall enjoy his own again'.

The outlook was bleak for the Protestants, James having dismissed the Protestant Chief Justice, Keating, from the Privy Council. It was rumoured that James had said that a Protestant stunk in his nostrils upon emerging from the first Mass celebrated in Dublin. Soon wild stories were circulating. There was the story of one Brown, a Protestant magistrate in County Cork, a wealthy man, who had been put on trial for resisting with force the Rapparees who had come to rob him. James arrived in Cork during the Assizes, and Brown expected a royal pardon in the event of his being convicted. He was sadly mistaken, for James let Brown be hanged and quartered.

There was the unfortunate Mr Maxwell, a Protestant of Queen's County who had been sentenced to death, who like Brown had tried to defend his house against Rapparees. His wife persuaded the sheriff to postpone the execution for fifteen days. She hurried to Dublin to beg mercy for her husband from James. The Irish nobles joined in the plea for mercy, but James told Mrs Maxwell that her husband must die, the sheriff being rebuked for his humanity. He was ordered to hang Maxwell.

All these stories were believed by the Protestants, and taken as proof of James's brutality and his vendetta against their faith. It was rumoured that the Catholics were committing great atrocities throughout the land. It was said that in Dublin no Protestant dare venture out after dark, and that several Protestants had been murdered. Protestant clergymen, too, went in fear of their lives and they were particularly at risk. Dr John Roan, Bishop of Killaloe was robbed of everything and Dr Hugh Gore, Bishop of Waterford, was stripped and beaten, having been surprised in his bed. Clergymen were waylaid as they went about their business. They were fired at and wounded, and in many cases narrowly escaped with their lives. Some were beaten with such severity that they died a short while later.

In Dublin, the soldiers considered it their duty to insult any Protestant clergyman. The scourge of all Protestants was Lord Galmoy, who eleven years earlier had been Chancellor of Oxford University. He was now riding north with his dragoons to guard the passes from Connaught into Ulster, riding on Hamilton's left flank. His troopers fell in with the wife of a Protestant clergyman who had fled to Ulster; they ravished her, one after another. They cut open her body, and left it exposed in a savage manner. Dragoons were rumoured to have committed all sorts of sexual outrages. Some were said to have broken into a Protestant house in Tipperary where they raped the owner's daughter before his eyes. Thirteen of them raped her while she was expiring, and three of them committed the crime whilst she was dead.

James heard about Richard Hamilton's setback at Coleraine, and he at once sent Berwick north to strengthen the position. One of the French Major Generals, Pusignan, was ordered up to Charlemont, and the king also despatched to Ulster several more regiments, and Avaux said that they plundered all that lay in their path. The plan was that Hamilton's forces, Pusignan's and the main body from Dublin, were to meet in the region of Strabane and Lifford. They would then proceed to force their way across the fords of the Rivers Mourne and Finn, which at Lifford unite to become the Foyle. James's forces would then march down the left bank of the Foyle to take Londonderry.

It was Lundy's decision whether he should march out from the city to contest the river fords or await the king's arrival at Londonderry. If he successfully contested the fords of Mourne and Finn, this would mean that the Protestants would come into possession of the fertile Laggan district, denying it to the enemy. The rest of the countryside had been laid waste and an army could not support itself upon it. The Catholics would have to retreat or starve. Lundy had now more troops at his command than the few hundred that existed last

December. There were now some thirty Ulster regiments represented in the garrison, and all the country had come to Londonderry as a last resort. From County Down had come Sir George Maxwell's regiment from Killyleagh, Sir John Magill's and Squire Hill's Hillsborough contingent. From County Antrim came the Ballymena men under Colonel Edmonstone. Another two regiments, Lord Blayney's and Audley Mervin's, had arrived from Armagh. Mountjoy's dragoons from Tyrone had ridden in from Newtownstewart. Hamill's regiment had marched in from Strabane; Colonel Chichester's from Dungannon. Squire Johnstone's horse came in from Caledon in County Tyrone. From Donegal came the Lagan horse and Squire Forward's horse from Burt and Inishowen. From County Londonderry, Kenny's Garvagh regiment rode in; from Coleraine came Parker; from Limavady and the Roe Valley came George Phillips. These were nearly all amateur levies, with little training and hastily recruited. Many 'regiments' were under strength, so much so that we hear that Lord Mount-Alexander's regiment of horse had now found himself commanding a force of some 7,000 men, reasonably well armed and not lacking in determination.

Rumours reached the city that great atrocities were being committed by the Catholic army. Galmoy's sex-maniac troops were on the rampage, and he found that Crom Castle, near Enniskillen, was held by a strong Protestant force under Colonel Creighton. He made two mock-up cannons nearly a yard long and about eight inches wide, each contraption being pulled by a team of eight horses. They made a great noise as if they were being drawn with great difficulty. Galmoy arrived outside the walls, and he could not resist the temptation to see if the cannons worked. He ordered one of them to be fired, which wounded a gunner. The garrison made a sally, and seized the other cannon and carried it away.

While this was going on, Gustavus Hamilton of Enniskillen managed to get more men into the castle there to reinforce the garrison, which had little artillery. He managed to obtain some long-barrelled fowling pieces, and one of these weapons nearly ended Galmoy's life. Galmoy had been standing on a hill drinking, when a shot from the walls shattered the glass in his hand and killed a man standing beside him. The garrison rushed out and killed thirty or forty of the besiegers and drove the rest from the trenches. Galmoy headed for Belturbet where he court-martialled two young Protestant officers, whom he had captured at Enniskillen. In exchange for the two young officers, Gustavus Hamilton had undertaken to release an Irish prisoner, Captain Brian Maguire. Hamilton released his prisoner, having been given to believe that the exchange was agreed, but then he promptly court-martialled them, sentencing them to death for high treason. Maguire interceded for them, but his plea was ignored. At this he resigned his commission and returned to prison at Crom Castle, swearing that he would no longer serve King James.

The Protestant prisoners, Charleton and Dixey were offered their lives if they renounced Protestantism and took service with King James. They refused and Galmoy had them hanged at an inn sign. The bodies were carried into the pub's kitchen, where the heads were cut off and kicked round the streets of Belturbet by Galmoy's troops before they were nailed on the market house. Galmoy then rode on towards Londonderry, terrorizing Omagh and hanging more people. The men of Londonderry were convinced that King William would not leave them to their fate, for on 21st March, Captain James Hamilton sailed into Derry in a ship called the *Deliverance*, with 8,000 muskets, 480 barrels of powder and £8,595 in cash. He was Richard Hamilton's nephew, but he stood firmly for the Protestant cause and was presently rewarded by William with a peerage, becoming Baron Mountcastle and Viscount Strabane. At length he succeeded to the Earldom of Abercorn.

While all this was going on, William kept his word, and on 12th March, more than a week before James Hamilton's arrival in the *Deliverance*, orders were issued from Whitehall for the despatch of strong reinforcements to Londonderry. It had been intended to send four regiments under command of Major General Percy Kirke, who was notorious for his treatment of Monmouth's rebels after Sedgemoor. Now he transferred his allegiance to William. James was bitter about this defection, for he had been generous to him whilst he was on the throne.

Kirke's appearance upon the Ulster scene was postponed until a later date. Only two infantry regiments were sent, the 9th and 17th Foot. Both regiments were encamped near Liverpool. Colonel John Cunningham of the 9th was junior in the army list to Colonel Solomon Richards of the 17th. But as he commanded the senior regiment, it was to him that the command of the expedition was given. Orders were addressed to him of 12th March, signed by Lord Shrewsbury, the Secretary of State, and said that he was to go without delay to the quarters of the regiment under his command, and make sure that it would be ready to march to Liverpool at a time that he should appoint.

He was to inquire what ships were available at Liverpool which would be able to sail to Londonderry. Cunningham would find 1,000 muskets, which were to be used to make good any deficiencies in the regiments, whilst the remainder should go to Londonderry to arm the local levies. At Chester, Cunningham would receive £2,000 which was to be used for the troops' subsistence "and for the defence of the place, in repairing and providing what shall be defective therein, and to such other uses as you with the Governor of the said city, with whom you are to entertain a good correspondence and friendship, shall find necessary for our service".

After preparations had been completed, Cunningham was to set sail for Londonderry and ascertain whether the city was still held by the Protestants, wind and weather permitting. He was to land his stores and ammunition at the city, and he was to give the Governor and the citizens an assurance that more help would arrive from England as speedily as possible. Furthermore he was to join in the Protestant cause at Londonderry and help them defend the place against the Catholics. He was to report periodically upon the situation at

Londonderry. He was to ascertain what food was needed per head of the citizens, so that stores would not be sent unnecessarily from England. He was also to report upon how James Hamilton had discharged his mission, and he was to report anything that he thought might be useful for the Protestant cause.

If it seemed unsafe for him to land his troops at Londonderry, he might land at Carrickfergus or even Strangford or in the last resort, return to Liverpool. The directive covered all eventualities, and was drafted by men who were not sure of the position at the city. Two days later a postscript was added, saying that Cunningham was to receive a further £2,000, £500 of which was to be paid to Governor Lundy in view of his good services to the cause, the balance earmarked for the general expenses of the expedition.

By April 3rd, the expedition had all been brought together at Liverpool, and Cunningham made his first attempt to sail for Londonderry, but was driven back to Hoylake by a westerly gale. It was not until 10th April that the expedition sailed with ten troopships escorted by the frigate *Swallow* under command of Captain Wolfranc Cornwall, RN. It took six days to sail to the Foyle; an uncomfortable voyage, for which the troops blamed the Collector of Customs at Chester. In August, Colonel Richard had told a House of Commons Committee that his men had been unable to lie down to sleep as no platforms had been provided. Other witnesses said that the biscuit was rotten and mouldy, having been at store at Chester Castle since Monmouth's rebellion four years previously. The cheese was good, but some of the beef stank so much that the men chose to drink sea water or their own urine. In such circumstances some of the troops died or were very ill. It was also revealed that Cunningham did not receive the full amount of money allotted to him for the expedition.

It was a race for Londonderry, with the English approaching by sea and the Catholics by land. Meanwhile the citizens of Londonderry were having second thoughts about the goodwill of Governor Robert Lundy. They had not questioned his authority when he ordered the abandonment of Coleraine, and for the garrison there to fall back upon Londonderry. The troops would be a useful addition to the city's military strength. Moreover the situation at Coleraine had been untenable. Lundy had told the Coleraine men that he was holding a year's stock of provisions at Londonderry, which he intended to reinforce with the large stocks of corn and hay he had seen along the road from Londonderry to Coleraine. Two weeks later Lundy was telling a very different story to Colonel Cunningham.

The first serious doubts about Lundy arose when he started to pull back the other forces from different parts of the province. They were to disband their positions and head for Londonderry. In mid-March, he ordered Colonel Stewart to withdraw from Dungannon. No one wanted to quarrel with Lundy, who had been recognized by the Northern Council as Commander in Chief of the north-west. A result of the disbandment of Dungannon was that a large number of stores fell into Catholic hands. Another result was that the Rev. George Walker arrived in the city.

Cavan and Monaghan were also disbanded, and the inhabitants setting fire to their houses and possessions rather than have them fall into the hands of the Jacobites. Lundy ordered Lord Kingston to abandon Sligo and fall back upon Derry. If Sligo had have been held, it would have been almost impossible for the Catholics to invade Ulster from the west. Kingston was very alarmed at Lundy's orders and set sail for England to tell of the serious turn of events.

It seemed as if Lundy was following one of the basic principles of war, namely the concentration of force principle. It should also be noted that he ignored Tyrconnel's order to send Mountjoy's regiment back to Dublin. The four mixed companies that until now had been kept outside the walls, were purged of Catholics and brought into Londonderry. They joined the two exclusively Protestant companies that had been admitted earlier. Soon the Protestants of the city were accusing Lundy of either indecision or of selling the city out to King James. It was pointed out that before the Break of Dromore, he had promised to bring reinforcements to Hillsborough, but he did not do this. Rumour said that he was willing enough to fight against Tyrconnel but not against King James, from whom he held his commission. At a later Parliamentary Commission, Daniel Sherrard said that Lundy had given promotion to a captain who had openly said that he would not serve King William and that he would not take pay for serving with King James. Protestants cried in alarm that Lundy's intention of concentrating Ulster's strength at Londonderry was because he wanted to tie the army neatly up for King James.

At length, James Hamilton arrived at Londonderry in the *Deliverance*. Hamilton's instructions were that he was not to hand over the arms and ammunition to Lundy until he had taken an oath of allegiance to William and Mary in the presence of the mayor or the chief magistrate. Colonel Cormac O'Neill, the Mayor, was absent on active service with the Irish army; his deputy, John Buchanan was suspected of being a Papist. It was decided that Lundy should be sworn on board the ship, which was anchored in the harbour. He would do this in the presence of James Hamilton.

When the Governor arrived at the harbour, he found Arthur Rawdon and others already in the ship, paying a social call on the ship's officers. They had to withdraw from the captain's cabin, and were told that Lundy and the others were discussing private business; they remained above deck with Captain Beverley until they were wet with rain, so that it was not known what transpired in the cabin.

Rumour quickly spread that Lundy had not taken the oaths of allegiance at all. The Parliamentary Committee a few months later held that Lundy had taken the oaths of loyalty to William and Mary on board the *Deliverance*. It seems likely that Lundy did take the oaths, for it meant that James Hamilton would have been party to a subterfuge. The Committee held that Colonel Stewart, Captain Henry Mervyn and Captain James Corry, were all there when Lundy took the oaths. Mervyn and Corry, all loyal Williamites, had both signed a certificate to this effect.

It appeared to the citizens of Londonderry that Lundy had been furtive about taking the oaths, and that he wanted to deny taking them at a future date, if King James succeeded in winning back his kingdom. Next day the oaths of loyalty were taken in Lundy's presence by the leading citizens and officers, and George Phillips made the suggestion that Lundy should take the oaths again, to let people's minds rest. Lundy refused, showing considerable anger at the suggestion, saying that since he had to taken the oaths on board the *Deliverance*, it was unnecessary to take them a second time. Most people were dissatisfied with Lundy for not taking the oaths a second time and in public. From this point onwards Lundy appeared to be a very suspicious character, full of ill intent and to be taken notice of.

Chapter 11

Irish Life

The British tried to justify their occupation of Ireland by saying that it would bring greater security for the motherland and bring in increased wealth. Ulster would be transformed into an obedient and law-abiding province and become a permanent source of income to the Crown. England would also be secure against foreign invasion and the threat of another 1641 rebellion would be put in the distance. The servitors would be able to give a reward to their king and the ex-soldiers who had fought against Tyrone would have a place in Irish society. It was a good thing to advance English civilization in Ireland. Protestantism would take the place of Popery and the Irish would be enlightened. All these arguments appealed strongly to King James, who now revealed himself to be the most keenest planters of them all, and he claimed that the Irish would be saved from their depravity to English 'civility'. The true religion of Christ would be established among men almost lost in superstition.

James said that the planning of the plantation should be beyond criticism, for foreigners might step in to take advantage and the disaffected at home might do likewise. It was also argued that a plantation in Ulster would help solve population problems in England. London, it was believed, was overcrowded, along with the rest of the country. Believing the capital's population problem might reduce the possibility of plague which from time to time took a heavy toll on its citizens, and sent the court hurrying to Windsor or Oxford. The same arguments were put forward for the colonization of Virginia, to which the first wave of colonists went just before the flight of the earls in 1607.

Francis Bacon, the Solicitor General, was very much interested in the plans for Ulster, and he submitted a memorandum on the subject to James, saying that the planatation in Ulster was much larger than the plantation of Virginia. Chichester said that he would rather "labour with his hands in the plantation of Ulster than dance or play in that of Virginia".

It was reckoned that the Ulster plantation would attract enough settlers from the mainland. Ulster was very fertile; it had many natural resources, it was close to Scotland and the north of England; rents were low and valuable privileges would be offered. Before the wars of the seventeenth and eighteenth centuries, the province, said Chichester, was quite inaccessible. Englishmen were sure that once the British settled in Ulster the land would be developed and that there would be a handsome yield on capital invested. O'Cahan's country was known to be fertile and pleasant, rich and fruitful as any land in Ulster. It had good grazing land for large numbers of cattle, sheep, pigs and small horses, known as garrons. There was arable farmland as well, suitable for growing oats, rye, barley and flax. The Route, in North Antrim, was said to be as good corn land as any in Ireland; there were wild animals galore, prized for their meat and skins; there was red deer, foxes, otters, martins and squirrels. Rabbits swarmed in the Magilligan sandhills and were highly prized for their fatness and sweetness. Thousands of wild fowl teemed along the coast and on the many loughs — swans, barnacle geese, teal, mallard, plover, herons and cranes. Salmon and trout were in abundance in the many rivers. The salmon fisheries on the Foyle and Bann were famous, and it was reckoned that these two rivers between them produced 120 tons of salmon a year. In one day in 1635 at Coleraine, sixty-two tons of salmon were taken. There was also an eel fishery on the Bann, where the river emerged from Lough Neagh, and its eels were reckoned to be the finest available. The sea around the coast swarmed with fish and the many seals produced a useful supply of train oil.

The only thing wrong with O'Cahan's country, as far as the English were concerned, was the presence of the O'Cahans themselves. Slate was scarce, but there was plenty of stone, lime, sand, clay and shells for building materials. The staple fuel was peat and was in the ground for the taking. There were plenty of woods, namely the Forest of Glenconkeyne 'well nigh as large as the New Forest in Hampshire; here there were great oaks, elms, ash and other trees, suitable for building both houses and ships. There was iron ore at the foot of Slieve Gallion, and the wood could be used for smelting it'. Ulster, it seemed, was literally a land flowing with milk and honey, for there were 'good Flockes of Sheepe . . . good horses . . . Cattle of infinite number . . . Bees . . . Fish'.

The English, however, did not think much of the natives, whose land they would now 'plant'. The Irish were a pastoral nomad folk, living by 'creachting', which involved driving their flocks and herds to the new pastures when the old ones were exhausted. Arable farming seemed primitive to English standards, for there were no enclosed fields. The Irish 'ploughed by the tail', fastening five or six horses or oxen to a short plough by the tail. When the tail became stripped of its hair, ploughing ceased, and fresh animals were used. The Irish thought that the idea of burning the straw from the corn rather than threshing it was a good one. The hay harvest was left over until the corn was in, so that the hay was usually ruined by rain. Few peasants took pains at arable farming unless he felt sure that he could reap what he had sown. Cattle were often driven off into hiding, and a standing crop was often at the mercy of an enemy.

Peaceful conditions were necessary for the successful sowing of crops. The dominant class amused themselves with fighting, a 'national' pastime. When they were not fighting they listened to the bards sing songs of war and stories about the ancestors of a clan. An Elizabethan Englishman noted that 'There are two sorts of people to be considered . . . the one called the Kern and the other the Chorle. The Kern bredd up in Idlenesse and Naturally inclined to Mischiefs and Wickedness, the Chorle willing to labour and take pains if he might peaceably enjoy the fruits thereof'.

There were few towns in Ulster, and the people lived in hamlets or clustered round the castles of the chiefs in beehive huts, with walls of wattle or clay and plaster, and roofed with thatch or turf. Few had windows or chimneys, and a fire burned in the middle of the hut, the smoke disappearing through a hole in the roof. The Gael wore a long woollen mantle, which served for all purposes and was essential to keep him warm in Winter, when they would often lie out in the bogs and woods. The honest Chorle might be willing to labour, but to the English the Irish seemed a gay, dashing, thiftless and handsome race, ignorant and barbarous, whose minds were full of superstition and other nonsense.

There was another side to the Irish, for they were people of great antiquity, both full of wit and brave, a people that had received Christianity for well over a thousand years; they were lovers of music, poetry and all kinds of learning. To the English, an Irish chieftain lived in dirt and squalor, his house crammed with cattle, pigs, dogs and a long line of dependants. His daughters crouched naked beside the hearth. The poet Spenser said that the Irish led a beastly life, living together with their beasts in one room and in one bed. Barnaby Rich, in his *New Description of Ireland* wrote that the Irish would 'rather still retain themselves in their shuttishness . . . in their uncleanliness . . . than they would take any example from the English, either of civility, humanity or any manner of decency'. He said that their personal habits were revolting; they thought it unlucky to keep their milking vessels clean, with the result that the butter was bad along with the bread.

The Irish did not consider themselves uncivilized, and one of their bards has painted a picture of Irish life. There were pretty maidens clad in silks and velvets, working at embroidery or walking hand in hand on green lawns, or listening to the harps of minstrels. Youths try out their steeds or burnish their weapons. Oars dip into the waters of Lough Erne and gay and happy bands go out hunting. Rich wines are brought from Spain and France and flow into silver and gold beakers.

The islands on the lakes of Enniskillen, which the bard was writing about, were magical places. However these gay and happy bands more often than not were not going out to hunt Englishmen, but to pillage and kill their fellow countrymen. Women and children were left to rue the passing of their menfolk. The young prince of Fermanagh was nothing more than a robber baron, a phenomenon which England had been freed from sometime earlier.

Irish society was in a state of arrested development and the world had moved forward without Ireland. The poet Spenser noted that Ireland had not yet emerged from the dark ages. Eachard said that the natural wild Irish were of middle stature, strong in body, of a wonderful soft skin and had tender muscles. They were said to be of a quick wit, careless of their lives, enduring travel, cold and hunger. They were also given to fleshy lusts. They took their religion lightly, but were kind and courteous to strangers, constant in love, impatient of abuse or injury, implacable in amity, and passionate in all their affections. They were charmed by music, especially with the harp and bagpipes, and many of them were very skilful. Their diet to him seemed to be out of place, if not disgusting. They fed on herbs, especially watercresses, upon mushrooms, shamrocks and roots. They delighted in butter tempered with oatmeal, and also dark milk, whey, beef broth and flesh, sometimes without any bread at all. Corn was laid up for the horses, which they took good care of. When they were hungry they tried not to eat raw flesh, after they had pressed out the blood. They drank large quantities of usquebaugh or aqua vitae.

As far as dress was concerned they commonly wore short jackets of wool. Breeches were plain and close to the thighs over which they wore a mantle of shag rugg deeply fringed, of many colours. They often slept with their mantle over them on the ground. For the most part they were bare headed, except when they put on a headpiece. Hair was worn long and they counted it a great ornament. The women were also very careful with their hair, especially if it were a golden colour and long. They adorned their heads with great quantities of fine linen, rolled up in wreaths.

The Irish, according to the English, were plainly a violent race, for their way of living was of a very odd sort. They were not usefully employed, for they were given to idleness and made little effort at anything; however they enjoyed their liberty. Their cows and cattle were their chief form of wealth and they held them in great esteem. They did not think much of stealing or committing robberies, which they carried out with great cruelty. When they set out on a robbery, they prayed to God that they would find a victim, and finding the victim, they said that it had come through God's will.

Murder and violence were considered no ways of displeasing God, for if it were a sin He would not have presented them with the opportunity to steal. They counted it a sin not to make use of an opportunity to rob. They claimed that this way of life was left to them by their fathers, and that the nobility should steal instead of earning their living by labour.

Before they sowed their corn, the wife or mistress of the house sent salt to the field. In the towns, when any magistrate entered first upon his office, the wives and daughters along the streets and out of the windows of the houses, bestrewed them and their followers with wheat and salt. At every third word they uttered an oath, as 'by the Trinity', 'by Christ', 'by Saint Patrick', or 'by Saint Brigid', 'by their baptism', 'by their Godfather's hand' and suchlike. If they swore by any great man and he foresworn, they forfeited a great sum of money or cattle to that same person whose name they used.

Superstition was rife; if their butter was stolen, they believed they could get it back by throwing some over the door into the fire. Chickens were protected from marauding bands by handing up the eggshells from which the chickens had been hatched. The Irish were very wary of people praising their livestock, and 'if any man befell that beast within three days later, they seek out him that praised him and then mumble the Lord's Prayer in his right ear'. When they

65

E

first saw the moon after the change, they bow the knee and say the Lord's Prayer, and then speak to the moon with a loud voice. They prayed for wolves, wishing them well, and they are not afraid to be hurt by them. When a horse died, they hung up his feet and legs in the house, and the hooves were esteemed as a holy and sacred relic. A woman or a witch that came to fetch fire on them on a May Day was counted as wicked.

The Irish attitude to death was highly amusing. When anyone lay dying, women were hired to stand at crossways, calling out upon the deceased with great cries and abundant expostulations why he should part from so many advantages. After he was dead, they kept mourning with loud howlings and clapping of hands together. When the corpse went forth they followed it with such a peal of outcries that a man would think that the quick as well as the dead were beyond recovery. They did not mourn less for those that were slain in battle or by robbery, though they believed that they had an easier death. They rallied on their enemies with spiteful words and continued for a long time great hatred against their kindred.

In warfare they used horsemen and soldiers set in the rearguard, which were called gallowglasses. They fought with sharp hatchets, and they used light-armed footmen called kerns, whose service was with darts and skeans. Shouts were given to every man going out of a gate, and was counted as fortunate. Bagpipes were commonly used instead of trumpets. They carried amulets and recited prayers and when there was a battle they cried as loud as they could "Phorroh!" Those who did not cry so loud would be suddenly taken from the ground and carried along the air into certain deserts and valleys, where they would eat grass, lap water, and have some use of reason, but not of speech; but with the help of hounds and hunters they should be brought home again.

Roman Catholicism was the religion of Ireland. In some respects the Irish were very devout, fasting every Wednesday and Saturday, and some of them fasting on Saint Catherine's Day and also on Christmas Day, whether they were sick or not. However in matters of divine service, they were very slack, for their vestments were foul and nasty, so much so that they would turn one's stomach. The altar was portable and polluted. The Mass book was all torn, the lead chalice without a cover, and the small vessels for wine made of horn. Priests were poor and in some respects were very mercenary; they made a great show of the canon law but had very little learning. Barnaby Rich was sharp in his criticism of Irish superstitions and ridiculed the celebrations that took place on saints' days. The Irish rattled and tinkled on pans and candlesticks; there was much strewing of herbs. He said that the Irish clergy were 'Our holy, holy brood of Jesuits, seminaries, friars and other such other do perform strange things, but specially for the increase and propagation of children, not a barren woman in an house where they be lodged'. However Eachard found grounds for hope, and said that 'the Irish had some industry and because of their intercourse with the English, they had acquired some degree of civilization, but in trade and learning'.

Chapter 12

The Battle of the River Fords

After the closing of the gates in December, David Cairns had headed for London to seek help. He managed to gain an interview with King William through the good offices of the Irish Society, and it was as a result of his efforts that the *Deliverance* brought supplies to Londonderry. Cairns returned to Derry after a journey from London taking four weeks, arriving in Londonderry on 10th April. This was about two or three weeks after Lundy had behaved suspiciously over the taking of the oaths of loyalty and a day after the refugees arrived at Londonderry from Coleraine. There was a good deal of confusion at this point in time. He came ashore some miles below the city, and as he hurried to the city it was to his surprise that he found some officers hurrying away from it. He learnt that Lundy had given some of them passes to leave, and had urged them to depart, speaking very pessimistically about the prospects of defending the place.

It was rumoured that Lundy meant to sell out the city to King James — this was the reason why some of them were leaving. Cairns continued his journey, hoping that he could change Lundy's mind or to help matters himself. Cairns carried with him a further directive, again signed by Lord Shrewsbury, which voiced concern about William's position in the course of events in Ireland, particularly for the province of Ulster, which he thought was capable of defending itself against the enemy. Secretary of State Shrewsbury said that two regiments were already to embark (this was Cunningham's force). They were sailing from Liverpool on the day that Cairns arrived in Londonderry with Shrewsbury's message. These two regiments would be followed by a considerable body, which would attempt to settle matters in William's Irish Kingdom, and in short safeguard Protestant interests. It was essential that Lundy stopped the deluge of Popery that threatened the faith and exercise great vigour.

Lundy was further encouraged by King William and it was promised that there would be rewards for the Governor's success, if this should attend him. Shrewsbury's letter was read out by Lundy at his Council of War, consisting of sixteen officers. Cairns was invited to the Council describing the preparations being made in England for the relief of Londonderry, and he urged that from now on no one should be permitted to leave the city. The Council then proceeded to draw up twelve Articles of War, to be read out to all the troops. The first article said that a bond was to be made between the officers and between all other ranks and signed by every man. 'None shall desert or forsake the service, or depart the Kingdom without leave of a Council of War. If any do, he or they shall be looked upon as a coward and disaffected to the service'. Other articles dealt mainly with the organization of the garrison and the levelling of old houses about the walls and ditches outside the gates. There was an order that upon the beating of the retreat every night, people were to go to their houses. The ninth article provided that a pair of gallows should be erected on one of the bastions, where the execution of traitors would take place. The final article laid down the weekly ration for every man, which was to be eight quarts of meal, four pounds of fish and three pounds of meat. Every soldier and NCO was to be given some free beer until money arrived to pay the soldiers.

When the articles were agreed, James Hamilton proposed that all those present should draw up and sign the 'mutual engagement', and when this was done the signatories said that they would stand by each other with their forces against the common enemy and not 'depart the Kingdom until matters were settled between themselves and King James'. There were twenty-two signatories in all, for three or four more officers joined the meeting. Amongst such names that signed were Lord Shrewsbury, Sir Arthur Rawdon, and James Hamilton. John Campsie's name, the Protestant Mayor, was missing; he had resumed office after the closing of the gates. He was mentally ill, and in place of his signature was Gervaid Squire, who, when Campsie died four days later, took up the office of Mayor and remained there throughout the siege.

A copy of the 'mutual engagement' was posted up on the wall of the market house. When it was read out next morning to the battalions on parade, it was seen to contain Lundy's signature, so that the men thought that he had at last come to his senses and was determined now to defend Londonderry!

On 13th April, a Saturday, the citizens of Londonderry, looking out across the Foyle from the walls, could see troops on the opposite bank, the vanguard of Richard Hamilton's force on its way from Coleraine to join the main body of the Irish army at the fords of Mourne and Finn. Hamilton fired a single cannon shot across the River Foyle, striking the bastion by the Ferry Gate; but it did not do much damage. The fire, to the consternation of the citizens, was not returned, for there was no ammunition available — so Daniel Sherrard told the Parliamentary Committee. This increased the citizens' dislike of Lundy, and voices were heard demanding that he go out and confront the enemy at the river fords. When these arguments were forced upon Lundy, he paid no attention, with the result that the Catholics had a day's march before them.

On 13th April, the Council of War, that had appointed Lundy as commander in the field, issued an order as a result of the pressure of public opinion:– "On Monday next, by ten o'clock, all officers and soldiers, horse, dragoons and foot, and all other armed men whatsoever of our forces and friends, enlisted or not enlisted, that can or will fight for their country and religion against Popery, shall appear on the ground near Cladyford, Lifford, and Long Causey as shall be nearest to their several and respective quarters, there to fight the enemy, and to preserve our lives and all that is dear to us from them".

Each man was told to carry with him at least a week's ration and as much fodder as possible for the horses. No detailed order of march was laid down; individual units and the leaving of the initiative to loyal commanders on the spot, led to confusion and disorder.

It was feared that Monday morning might be too late for the offensive — so Cairns and others believed. Lundy was pressed to get his men out at the river fords by Sunday evening at the latest. It was essential that he should be there himself; but Lundy replied that he had already issued the necessary orders and was not going to change them. George Walker's entreaties were also brushed aside. Walker had been out at the river fords and received intelligence that the Catholics were drawing closer to Londonderry. Walker rode with all haste to the city to give Lundy an account of matters, but he only said that it was a false alarm.

Mayor Stroud suggested that agricultural implements should be placed in the rivers to trip the Catholics' horses, but his advice was not taken. It so happened that the river fords were swollen with rain and his idea would have been to no avail, so that the horses would have to swim across. However Lundy had posted cavalry vedettes at the fords. Four days earlier he had reinforced them by the dragoons from Coleraine, who had brought with them meal and other provisions.

On Sunday, 14th April, David Cairns' need for haste was turning out to be correct, for on that day the Catholics made an almost unopposed crossing of the Mourne, which was the more southerly of the two rivers. They made ready to cross the Finn, to put themselves in a position to march on Londonderry.

There were three possible crossing places; Lifford, Cladyford, about three miles upstream from Lifford, and Long Causey, about another mile further north. They attempted to cross Cladyford on the 14th, but this was successfully repulsed by the garrison. The Protestants, led by Captain Crofton and Mayor Hamilton, fought through the night and inflicted heavy casualties upon the Catholics. However the Protestant weakness was already showing, for there was a shortage of ammunition, with Adam Murray's troop being sent into battle with only three rounds to each man, and with Stroud's men being forced to retire because of a lack of powder. There were reinforcements on their way from Londonderry and the Protestant outposts had done good work, so there was reason to suppose that the river fords might be held.

The Catholics now proposed to make a crossing at Cladyford in the face of vastly superior Protestant numbers, for by 15th April, Protestant troops were beginning to arrive on the scene from the city. Berwick, on the field, said that the attack at Cladyford was made with no less than 350 infantry and about 600 cavalry. He put the number of Protestants at about 10,000. Mackenzie puts the odds in favour of the Protestants at ten to one, Nicholas Plunket, the Jacobite, at seven to one and Captain Ash, the Protestant diarist, at five to one. However the

Protestants had a desperate lack of ammunition. Lord Blayney told the Parliamentary Commission that the Protestants cried out that they wanted powder, once they were ready for battle. Most of them wanted arms. Lundy's orders had been vague, for all the Protestants had been told was that they were to appear before the ground at Lifford, Cladyford and Long Causey. Markers may have been put out, so that the Protestants could find their respective quarters more easily; but the picture is one of confusion in the Protestant camp, with no clear idea of what they should do or where they should go.

Richard Hamilton had been given the task of forcing the passage at Cladyford, and he saw that the Protestants were completely disorganized. Seeing this, Berwick ordered his men to swim across the river, but there was no ford at the point he had chosen. There was only a partially demolished bridge, beside which the Protestants held out on the far bank. The Protestants were driven from their trenches by the fire of the Catholic muskets, and at this the Jacobites plunged into the river and proceeded to swim across, together with their horses, with each trooper towing along an infantryman, clinging to the horses' tails or manes.

The Protestants fired at the Catholics, but to no avail, and the Irish were across the Finn with the loss of only two privates and one officer, Major Mangle, who fell headlong from his horse in the mid-stream and who was shot at Longford Bridge.

The Catholics emerged bedraggled from swimming across, and they were met with more gunfire, and they were afraid that the Protestants might catch them unawares, with only wet gunshot in their muskets. All along the Protestant line there were desperate shouts for powder, and they had scarcely any ammunition at all, wet or dry. The Catholics started to patch up the broken bridge, which they started to cross, at the sight of which the Protestants fled in alarm with shouts of "To Derry! To Derry!" This was not all, for the Catholics now succeeded in again crossing the Finn, this time at Lifford, a few miles downstream. They were led by the senior officer of the French military mission, sixty-two-year-old Lieutenant General de Rosen, a soldier of fortune from the Russian province of Livonia. He had entered the French service as a private soldier, and he at length was commissioned, showing much courage and marrying well. He served with enough distinction to reach the rank of Major General and to be made Colonel General of the French cavalry. Berwick found him intolerable, but admitted that he was an excellent officer, capable of great bravery and application. However Berwick said that he was not capable of commanding an army, for he always feared accidents. In private life de Rosen led a magnificent style, but he was subject to passions, verging on madness, and in these moods no one could reason with him.

Rosen's idea of how to deal with hostile populations had been learnt in the Thirty Years' War. He had a savage temper, his manners were coarse, his language a strange jargon made up of various dialects of French and German. He had a fierce appearance, so much so that one would be scared to run into him after dark.

He was a man of great energy and courage, which he now displayed at Lifford. At first he thought that a crossing was impossible, for the river was in full flood. He had only two troops of horse and one of dragoons. The Protestants, on the far bank, were ten times as numerous; they were entrenched in a small fort and had some artillery. When he saw the Protestants retreating from Cladyford, he seized his chance, and he bravely attempted the passage, the troops swimming the river with de Rosen at their head. The Protestants fled at the first charge, and he pursued them for three or four miles, killing many of them. The Protestants had stayed long enough to fire only a single round before joining the rest of their fleeing comrades from Cladyford, in the flight back to Londonderry.

The Catholics pursued the Protestants, and although unable to catch up with their horse, overtook and killed about 400 of their infantry, the rest taking refuge in bogs into which the horses could not follow. The pursuit continued for about five miles until Hamilton called a halt and until reinforcements could be brought up. This gave the Protestants the opportunity to get safely back to the city.

It was now a fact that a handful of bold Catholics had brought about the complete rout of the Protestants, and it had been the 'Break of Dromore' all over again. There was even less excuse for this, for the Protestants had vastly superior numbers. But the Protestants which fled from the scene were to be the same stalwart souls that would defend their city against King James, and to bring this to a successful conclusion. The Protestant rout at Lifford and Cladyford could be explained by the fact that the Protestants were expecting open field warfare, and that they were in a better position to defend their city from behind the walls. After the siege, the Protestants soon developed an aptitude for brisk skirmishing.

The main cause of the stampede back to Londonderry, was the Protestants' inability to organize themselves and the lack of any proper orders, either before or during fighting. The Protestants, in response to the Council of War's orders, had arrived upon the scene in a higgledy-piggledy fashion, lacking both arms and ammunition. Lundy had been looked upon as the Commander in Chief, and the Parliamentary Commission said that 'there was no sort of care taken, few of the men having Powder, nor was there three Guns fired before they were all routed'.

Lundy cannot escape responsibility, but his lack of decision was soon seen as betrayal by the injured pride of the citizens. Cairns did not trust the 'traitor', and he told the Parliamentary Committee that in some way the Catholics had been informed of Protestant intentions, because the Catholics had marched to the place where the Protestants were to meet. Walker in a letter written from Londonderry after the siege had said that Lundy gave the Irish commander a signal to come over and then ran away. Joseph Bennett, another witness at the Parliamentary Committee, said he was not sure if Lundy gave a signal or not when the Irish tried to cross at Gladyford.

It is unlikely that Lundy was in league with the enemy, but rather his leadership at the fords was lamentable. He had lacked all sense of urgency and

71

he had ignored the advice of David Cairns and others, who recommended a speeding up of the advance to the river fords. Lundy was lethargic and this was interpreted as treachery, for if he had marched out his army on Sunday the 14th, the Catholics might not have so easily got over at Lifford and Cladyford. It was not until Monday that he marched out his troops to the fords, and he ignored one of the basic principles of war, which was to get to the scene of battle as fast as possible. Moreover he had made no reconnaissance of the river fords. In Colonel John Mitchelburne's play *Ireland Preserved* (who presently joined George Walker as joint Governor during the siege), it was suggested that Lundy was not present at the river fords at all, but remained in Londonderry, drinking himself into a stupor. A dialogue takes place between three characters standing on the bank of the Finn: Fergus, the town-major Granado, who is Mitchelburne himself, and Monrath, who in real life was Captain Adam Murray:–

Fergus: See how regular and formidable Lieutenant General Hamilton advances, that has not half the number of men we have, when at the same time our Governor lies sitting and drinking in Derry . . . sends us twelve miles from Derry as the Governor of Colerain sent us twelve miles from thence, to be cut off by the enemy's horses and dragoons.

Granado: No, Fergus, he is safe and we are not. Lieutenant General Hamilton and he combine against us and seek our ruin. We have enemies both before and behind us. We are betrayed, sold.

Monrath: 'Tis a most deplorable case to think how we are served. The Lord Kingston is within twenty miles with 3,000 foot and 1,000 horse to join us, yet this treacherous Governor and his friends are not content to get this Kingdom to themselves but destroy us root and branch. Thus are we scattered through the country, that the enemy shall have little or no opposition.

It might have been better indeed if Lundy had remained behind in Londonderry drinking, but there is no doubt that he was present at Cladyford and that he arrived there just when the Protestant defence was starting to disintegrate. Walker says that when the Irish succeeded in crossing the Finn, the Governor gave a great oath, and seeing that his men would not fight, ran away himself. This does not exclude the fact that the Protestants were very willing and able to fight, and if they had had better leadership, their reputation would have been saved. Bennett said that Lundy was heard saying, as he fled, "You are all lost, shift for yourselves", and Colonel Chichester testified that he met Lundy running from the pass, and told him that he should give more positive orders or all would be lost. Lundy replied that Londonderry was his post and made his way there as fast as he could. Lundy later denied that he had said this to Bennett, but admitted that he had run away with all the rest; he denied that he had given any positive orders to run away. Now would he deny that once he got safely back to the city, that he gave orders for the gates to be closed, thereby excluding many of his own men — the number put at between 4,000 to 8,600 men, so that if the Catholics had pursued, all these men would have been lost. Many of them made their way round the city to the peninsula of Inishowen, where many of them were killed by the natives.

It was at this point in time that the Reverend George Walker managed to persuade one of the sentries to admit him to the city. The gates were closed again and were only opened when a Captain Skeffington pointed a pistol at the sentry and threatened to burn the gates down. Lundy's explanation for the closing of the gates was that keeping out the 4 or 5,000 Protestants would save provisions in the town. Now came good news and it seemed that Londonderry would still enjoy the luck it enjoyed when it kept out Antrim's Redshanks in December. Word spread that there were ships anchored in the Foyle, for by the narrowest margin the English had won the race to reach Londonderry first. Cunningham's fleet had just arrived.

Chapter 13

Lundy the Traitor

While the Protestants were meeting disaster at the fords of the Finn, Cunningham's fleet arrived in the Foyle on 15th April. At ten o'clock that morning, a messenger was put ashore at Greencastle to send a message to Lundy and to await his orders. Cunningham's flotilla then sailed slowly up the lough and by 2 p.m. were off Greencastle. Cunningham by now had learnt that the garrison had marched out to engage the Catholics at the river fords. He received no reply to the letter sent from Greencastle and landed a second courier, who carried another sensible message to Lundy. The message was written on board the *Swallow*, near Redcastle, at two in the afternoon. It said that Cunningham had heard that Lundy had taken to the field, and that there were two well-disciplined regiments on board that would join him in two days at the least. He said that the regiments would be of great use on any occasion, and would encourage Lundy's raw recruits. It was recommended that Lundy should only stop the passages at the fords of Finn until Cunningham could join him. He said that William and Mary had left matters entirely in Lundy's hands, and that he — Cunningham — would willingly obey him in all matters. It was signed, John Cunningham.

The fleet reached Culmore by 9 p.m., where it dropped anchor for the night, for the tide had failed. Major Zachariah Tiffin was sent by land to Londonderry, now that there was still no word from Lundy. Cunningham was asking once again for orders — for the best method of getting his two regiments into the city. Along the road Tiffin ran into a messenger from Lundy, bringing Lundy's reply to the two letters. Tiffin made the man turn back and accompany him to the city. Here he met the Governor, who now added a postscript to his letter. In the letter Lundy said that he had arrived back from the river fords sooner than expected, and asked Cunningham to send his troops to Londonderry as soon as possible and to watch that they were not surprised. They would find ample accommodation in the city. It was signed, Your faithful servant, Robert Lundy, and dated 15th April 1689. After Tiffin's arrival in Londonderry, Lundy added a postscript. It informed Cunningham that since Major Tiffin's arrival, Londonderry would fall to the enemy without an immediate supply of provisions. If Cunningham did not send his men sometime tomorrow, it would not be in his power to send them at all. The postscript was signed R.L.

Tiffin reported to Cunningham that Londonderry had not ten days' provisions for 3,000 men, which was Lundy's claim. Affairs in the city were in great confusion. It was suggested that Cunningham should leave his troops anchored at Culmore and come himself to Londonderry to discuss the next steps in a Council of War. Cunningham readily complied with this suggestion, for he was compelled to follow Lundy's directions in all matters relating to the king's service. Next morning, together with Colonel Richards and three or four officers from each regiment, and a Captain Cornwall to represent the Royal Navy, he arrived in Londonderry, where they went first to the Governor's house. Here they met the local gentry and garrison officers. Colonel Richards noticed, according to his evidence he gave later to the Parliamentary Committee, that Lundy and he whispered something together at a window, but did not know what they said. On Lundy's suggestion, the meeting adjourned to the Council Chamber where, according to Richards, Lundy refused to admit officers who had attended other Councils, particularly Colonel (Francis) Hamilton, Colonel Chichester, Major Walker and Major Baker. Lundy's plan was that he should exclude any diehards, but Walker was not to be kept out so easily. Colonel Chichester and Major Walker tried to thrust their way into the room, but Lundy ordered them to be kept out, saying that the Council was a select company. The Council was indeed select, for the only ones who attended this meeting apart from Lundy himself, were Lord Blayney, Captain Chidley Coote, and James Hamilton. These people Walker described as being totally unacquainted with conditions in the town or with the temper of the people. The records of the Parliamentary Committee are the only sources available describing what happened at this meeting; in particular the evidence given by Colonel Solomon Richards. Richards cuts a more responsible figure than the others, but he would have been concerned to justify his opinion to the Committee.

The Council appears to have opened with Cunningham handing to Lundy the instructions he had been given by William, as well as a further letter from the king to Lundy, which confirmed the news already brought by Cairns that further reinforcements were on their way. Meanwhile, William expected Lundy to make the most of the situation at Londonderry and defend the place. William expected that Lundy, Cunningham and Richards would co-operate, and that 'the city will continue under our obedience until upon the arrival of an army, which we are sending from England, all things shall be in such a posture as that we may, with the blessing of God, restore in a short time our Kingdom of Ireland to its former peace and tranquillity'.

However Lundy's mind seems to have been already made up. He at once proposed that Cunningham's two regiments should be sent back, and that the town should be surrendered, saying that there was not a week's or ten days' provisions left. Richards was the only dissenter, by his own account, and said that quitting the town was like quitting the Kingdom. This provoked Major Tiffin to rise up and swear that he would be hanged for no man's pleasure. Someone else — Richards thought that it might be Cunningham —said that he would go home, no matter who would be displeased. This ended the discussions, for the Council unanimously resolved that the best course of action was for the troops to return to England rather than stay at Londonderry, which was not victualled from the country, especially as Lundy claimed when the enemy was nearly at the gates with 25,000 men.

The members of the Council agreed and all present signed a resolution that they would quit the town, and got down to the business of drafting a note of surrender. Walker wrote later that there was no doubt that upon surrender of the town, King James would grant a general pardon and order restitution of all that had been plundered from them. Some were influenced by Lundy's policies to surrender; others refused and many were hostile to him and were going to hang the Governor and his Council.

Lundy feared that the people might get wind of what he was planning and compelled the members of the Council to take an oath of secrecy. This was rejected when it was opposed by Richards, but what they resolved upon amounted to the same thing, namely not to reveal what had transpired at the meeting. Soon the Council was propagating shameless lies, and it claimed that when Cunningham's party left the city, it was only going to the ships at Culmore to bring up the troops. The people were curious at what had transpired at the meeting and the Council said that the troops were to be landed immediately and brought to the city. The subterfuge was in vain, for the cat was let out of the bag almost at once by the secretary, that silent figure at meetings who never speaks, on this occasion a man named John Mogridge, whom Walker, with his usual bizarre spelling, calls 'Machridge', and wrongly describes as the Town Clerk. John Mogridge was a city burgess, who had been pressed into service to act as secretary to the Council of War. He felt under no obligation to keep Lundy's secret, and he felt obliged to reveal the proceedings of the Council, so that Londonderry should not fall into the hands of James, but he was also resolved not to make it too public. There was an immediate outburst of popular rage, and the information caused great upheaval in the city, which had ill effects upon the Governor and his Council, for the people wanted Lundy lynched.

Adam Murray now steps into the scene, and he proceeded to lead the citizens. He was a young Ulster-Scot, who in peacetime, had worked on his father's farm at Ling, a few miles south-east of Londonderry, in the valley of the River Faughan. He had fought bravely at the battle of the river fords, in command of a body of yeoman cavalry. After that he had taken his men round the city and down to Coleraine, for there was no forage for his horses at Londonderry. Somehow he learnt about the Council's intentions. He at once set out for Londonderry with his men. He had got as far as Pennyburn Mill when he met with a kinsman, bringing him a request from the Council. Pennyburn Mill was within sight of the walls. It was requested of him 'that he should immediately upon sight thereof withdraw his men to the back of the hill, out of the view of the city'. Murray was informed that the first of the Catholic troops were starting to arrive at the Upper Strand, and that the sight of his troops might upset Lundy's plans for surrender.

Murray learnt that the citizens wanted him to come into the city to help thwart Lundy's plans for surrender and to head the opposition to the Governor, for if he did not, then Londonderry would surely fall to the Catholics. Murray hastened to the city, only to find Shipquay Gate closed in his face. Walker, who appears at this point not to have made up his mind, was sent to reason with Murray. Walker, leaning over the parapet, suggested that he should be hauled up on a rope over the walls. Murray refused to enter the city in such an undignified manner, and made it plain that he would enter the city with his men or not at all.

James Morrison ordered that the gates should be opened to Murray. Murray found that the great majority of citizens and soldiers were against the idea of surrender, and he therefore encouraged them to stand firm, assuring them that more help would soon be on its way from England. He promised to stand by them, and he insisted that they must eject Lundy and his 'false cabal'. He said that all who agreed with him should wear white brassards on their left arms. Soon thousands were displaying the armbands and proclaiming their determination to hold the city. They heaped imprecations upon Lundy's plans to surrender the city. They were determined not to 'yield the town to popery'.

Lundy, after Murray had made his way to the Council Chamber, invited him rather nervously to join the meeting. He hoped that Murray would use his influence to persuade the citizens to agree to a surrender. He accused the Governor of either being a fool or a knave, and in this he was supported by Lieutenant Cook from Lisburn. He pointed out that Lundy had failed to secure the river fords, and that he had failed to supply ammunition to the garrison who were willing and able to use it, and had failed to secure Long Causey and Carrigans, which could have been held with only a few men. As yet he did not know of the deception Lundy had practised over the English colonels, and he could have added this to his list of charges. The poem spoke of Lundy's incompetence:–

Then unto Lundy all in anger fly
Of treachery I now to you impeach
Both to the Protestants and to our King —
A popish reign upon us you would bring
You left Tyrone unto the enemy,
At Cladyford you made our arms fly.
And now you're plotting to betray the town
By a capitulation of your own.
Therefore lay down your pow'r for we will choose
Such loyal men will oppose our foes
Lieutenant Cook, who from fair Lisburn came,
Courageously stood forth and said the same.

The Governor and Council yielded to Murray, and Lundy's reign was over in Londonderry. Lundy and his men now decided to 'retire', finding that their

77

services were no longer wanted. Some of them made off to the ships at Culmore, but Lundy himself could not so easily escape, for he was the leader of the 'traitors'. He kept to his bedchamber, where a guard of his own Redcoats was posted to protect him against the fury of the citizens. Meanwhile the garrison had unanimously chosen Major Henry Baker and the Reverend George Walker, who also held the local rank of major, as their Governors. Walker and Baker, despite their brush over the walls, were not accused of defeatism. Both had been excluded from Lundy's Council meeting with the English officers. Despite all that had happened, their first action was to invite Lundy to resume the Governorship, but he refused. They then sent an emissary to Culmore to invite Cunningham to become Governor, whose business they thought it was to look after them. Cunningham thought that it was his duty to obey Lundy's order, and he did not take up the position. It was only now that Baker and Walker fully accepted the Governorship of the garrison. They at once arranged for the escape of Lundy, who might well have been lynched if he had been caught out of doors. They arranged his escape because of the office he had borne, which made it a duty on them to do all to help him. Lundy, eager to escape the tumult, seized upon the opportunity of escape. Baker and Walker persuaded him to disguise himself as a soldier, and in a sally for the relief of Culmore, he passed by with some match on his back, and thus got to the shipping. Match, to make his disguise more convincing, was the tow that was used to fire the matchlock musket, but many writers later interpreted it as matchwood, which explains why his effigy, which is burnt on the walls, is equipped with a bundle of 'scallops', the local name for faggots of firewood. Tradition states that he escaped from Londonderry by shinning down a pear tree growing against the city's east wall, and Macaulay, visiting the city in the '40s, met people who claimed to have eaten pears from the tree.

Lundy now disappeared from the scene at Londonderry, but not from the pages of history. His disguise took him safely to Culmore, where he took ship for Scotland; he was at once arrested and put in the Tower of London upon suspicion of treasonable practises against His Majesty's Government. He was summoned to appear before the Parliamentary Committee. All his claims and accounts of his behaviour were unconvincing. He told the Parliamentary Committee that he had estimated the amount of supplies of food at Londonderry out of good faith, but Cornet Nicholson said that there were ample supplies and provisions; every house was well stocked and that there were boats coming daily. There was sufficient at this time for three months' provisions for 3,000 men, as Lundy himself had told Lord Blayney a little while before. Blayney, present at the Council meeting, does not appear to have challenged Lundy's story, probably because he had acquiesced in Lundy's policy of surrender. Sir Arthur Rawdon, who had not acquiesced, told the Committee that Lundy had told him, two days before the arrival of Cunningham's ships, that the town had ample provisions for three months for 6,000 men. All that Lundy could do was deny the charges laid before him.

At the Parliamentary Committee the careers of Colonels Cunningham and Richards were terminated, and in the language of the day they were 'broken'. The verdicts seem harsh, particularly in the case of Richards, and presumably such action was taken to encourage others to do better. The Committee decided that Colonel Lundy should be sent over to Londonderry to stand trial for the treason laid against him, but this never happened. Lundy still had influence in England, particularly with Lord Melvill, to protect himself standing trial, and he now received support from an unexpected quarter. The siege was over and Walker, who had now been welcomed in London as an heroic figure, came to Lundy's defence. He was strongly opposed to the Committee's suggestion. He said that Lundy still had friends in Londonderry and that he might not be convicted; furthermore most material witnesses against him had not left the city. So it was all swept under the carpet, and Lundy was released on bail, and not so many years later was found back in the service of the Crown. In the War of the Spanish Succession he helped to defend Gibraltar against the French and Spaniards and in 1707, as 'Adjutant General of the King of Portugal's forces in the Queen of England's pay', he was taken prisoner, perhaps at the battle of Almanza. He was released in exchange for twenty men and allowed to return to England. By 1717 he was dead.

Nearly 300 years later, Lundy's behaviour at Londonderry remains despicable. Adam Murray was probably close to the truth in saying that Lundy was either a fool or a knave. Perhaps he was a defeatist, or maybe a realist, who wished to avoid senseless bloodshed in a cause in which he thought was lost. Perhaps he was always secretly loyal to King James? He had received his commission from James, and perhaps he was always disloyal to William to whom he claimed he had taken the oaths of loyalty aboard the *Deliverance*. Macaulay took a generous view and said that his conduct was 'rather to be attributed to faint-heartedness and to poverty of spirit than to zeal for any public cause'.

It is probable that Lundy told Cunningham lies about the state of supplies, in order to persuade him to leave before the English helped in a futile resistance to the Jacobites. On the other hand there is the evidence of Cornet Nicholson, who testified that upon the arrival of the Irish army outside the walls, he met an old acquaintance, a Protestant minister by the name of Whitloe, and whispered to him that Lundy was going to surrender the city to the enemy. It seems that Lundy was not a traitor, but a man of poor spirits and will. The postscript to the letter he wrote to Cunningham on the evening of 15th April, that the soldiers should be landed immediately, do not sound like the words of a traitor.

Next morning he tried to persuade Cunningham to keep the troops on the ships and to take them back to England. Why did Lundy change his mind during the night? Perhaps his nerve finally broke as he reflected upon the humiliation of the river fords and realized his ineptitude as a General. He had never commanded more than a few hundred men as a Lieutenant Colonel, and very seldom did he command them in battle. He had found himself utterly incompetent in commanding several thousand troops in the conflict of the river fords. He had asked his kinsman Melvill if he would not have returned to Great Britain if he had intended to be loyal to William and Mary. He said that he would have joined the Irish, from whom he could have expected protection, if not reward. Why had he still support at Londonderry when the siege was over? Walker had said that he had enough support to ensure acquittal. Why was he so soon again employed in the Crown's service? On the other hand Lundy's actions can be explained by the supposition that he was a traitor to King William and a Jacobite throughout. There is the 'Dropping Correspondence', which is preserved in the Armagh Library, which was first published thirty years ago in C D Milligan's history of the siege of Londonderry. The chief witness here is Captain Charles Kinaston, one of three envoys sent by Lundy to negotiate with Cornet Nicholson's friend, a clergyman called Whitloe. Lundy had been ousted by Murray's coup d'état before Kinaston had set out on his mission. Lundy, safely in his quarters, had asked to see Murray, but Kinaston cautiously consulted with the new Governor, Henry Baker, who encouraged him to see Lundy with the hope of finding out about some of his roguery. This he certainly did, for Lundy, after praising Kinaston, told him that he was going to let him into a great secret, which he insisted upon, despite Kinaston's unwillingness to listen. The Captain was to tell James, whom Lundy referred to without as 'the King' that he — Lundy — had managed affairs at the river fords properly and to King James's advantage. He had misrepresented the state of the garrison to Cunningham and thus had prevented the English regiments leaving the town; he had produced a letter forged by himself to the Council, but purported to be written by Cunningham, which advised the immediate surrender of the town as it was in no fit condition to hold out until help arrived from England.

Kinaston goes on to say that he had delivered the message as requested and that James had commented "Alas, poor men". He was satisfied that he had done Lundy all the service that he could. Kinaston seems to have invented all this, for malice or some other reason, but that would seem to be the end of the matter. Lundy appears from the start to have been a traitor to William, although one wonders why he escaped to Scotland, with his inevitable arrest instead of joining the Jacobite army. Why did he still have supporters in Londonderry when the siege was over? Why was he so soon back into the Crown's service? Perhaps he did not know which king would be the winner, and that he was trying to hedge his bets?

Today, Orangemen in Ulster have no doubt about Lundy, for to them Lundy was symbolic with being a traitor to the Protestant cause. He has become Londonderry's Guy Fawkes. On the closing of the gates, each year, his effigy, sixteen feet tall, weighing almost a ton and wearing a black uniform with gold epaulettes, is burnt on a bonfire on the walls. Upon its breast the guy bears the inscription 'Lundy the Traitor' and upon its back 'The End of All Traitors'.

Chapter 14

Londonderry is Organized

Henry Baker and George Walker were men of very different character, and they now took charge of the organization of Londonderry for the siege. Henry Baker was about forty-two and came of an English family, which had settled in Ireland at the beginning of the century, and had acquired estates in County Louth. It was in Louth that Henry was living at the end of 1688, when he decided to fight for the Protestant cause. During the retreat from Dromore to Coleraine he had shown great courage and a gift for leadership. This made him an obvious choice for the Governorship. Most people had a good word to say for Henry Baker. He died during the course of the siege. He was not able to write an account of the siege as George Walker did, and it is the clergyman that is remembered to history.

George Walker was a year or so older than Baker, and Macaulay believed that he was an old man, together with the Dictionary of National Biography. It was said that he was born in 1618, and thus seventy years old at the time of the siege. Macaulay uses such expressions as 'an aged clergyman', 'old Walker', 'his advanced age' and 'this brave old man'. There is now little doubt that Walker was born in 1646. C D Milligan has tracked down a reference in a report of a lawsuit in 1679 to a witness describing him as 'George Walker of Dungannon, clerk, aged thirty-three'. All accounts and portraits show Walker as a man in the prime of life and when he made his triumphal visit to England after the siege, a London Newsletter noted that he had been under great strain.

Walker came of a Yorkshire family and both his father and grandfather, who was the family pioneer in Ulster, had held rectorships in the diocese of Derry. His father, the elder George, fled to England in '41 during the rebellion, and did not return to Ulster until after the Restoration. He eventually became Chancellor of Armagh and Rector of Kilmore. George Walker must have been born in England during the period of exile, but seems to have eventually returned to Ulster with his father. He is almost certainly the George Walker who matriculated from Trinity College, Dublin, in 1662. He then took holy orders and nothing more is heard of him until 1688. He became Rector of Donoughmore, near Dungannon, in County Tyrone.

Tyrconnel's threat to the Irish Protestants became unmistakable. Walker then raised a volunteer regiment at Dungannon to defend the Protestant cause. He

F

always preferred the church militant to divine right and passive resistance. The men throughout the siege complained of a want of powder, but Walker got a bag of mustard seed, which was laid upon the carriages, which looked like a bag of powder and immediately gave a signal to the soldiers. Walker brought to Londonderry an implacable hatred of Popery and of Popes, and words to support it, together with a gift for organization and undoubted courage.

Walker had his critics within the walls, the bitterest of which was John Mackenzie, the Presbyterian minister of Derryloran. He was chaplain to Walker's own regiment at Londonderry and had hardly a good word to say for him. Walker's tendency was to take too much credit for himself, and this provoked Mackenzie's animosity. Walker tended to give too much credit to the Anglicans, and to give too little credit to the Presbyterians, pressing them to great lengths. Mackenzie started the rumour that Walker was in fact never Governor at all, but only a kind of superior quartermaster, who had been personally chosen by Baker to act as his assistant for stores and provisions. This was his main responsibility, but he also found time to command a regiment of troops. In *Ireland Preserved*, where he appears under the name of 'Evangelist', he is called 'commissary for the stones'.

Mackenzie also admits that as well as Baker, Walker was designated the title of Governor. The title of Governor, he says, was understood with reference to the stores. Mackenzie further says that Walker, in his account of the siege, is misleading about his role, for he claims all the credit for leadership during the siege. Mackenzie says that he fooled the world that he had been Governor and saviour of Londonderry. He compared him to the English Rogue, Spanish Gusman and Crafty Clansay, and charges Walker with being a confidence man. If he was Governor of the garrison he was such a person whose authority was insignificant. Mackenzie was the only contemporary to deny Walker the title of Governor; however many later Presbyterian writers made the same claims. In 1887, Dr Thomas Hamilton wrote that Walker had charge of the stores and oversaw the weighing and serving out of the bread and meat to the garrison, and with the military matters he had simply nothing to do with them. He was certainly not Governor, so these theories state. Dr A F Moody, fifty years later, suggested that Walker was a 'stage' character, and this conclusion undoubtedly comes from the account of himself with the confidence that comes from looking back at the event. However Moody did not suggest that Walker was a fraud, but said that he probably came to believe in the legend of himself in his own lifetime. All this is based upon Mackenzie, but there is a lot of contemporary evidence to the contrary, for example the *Londerias*, whose author was in Londonderry throughout the siege, for

> . . . then all with one consent
> Agreed upon this form of Government:
> Baker and Walker Governors they chose
> And formed eight regiments to oppose the foes.

Thomas Ash records in his diary that the government of the city was bestowed upon two worthy gentlemen, viz., Henry Baker and George Walker. Joseph Bennett says in his *True and Impartial Account* that after Lundy's downfall the city unanimously chose Mr George Walker, clerk, and Lieutenant Henry Baker their Governors. Bennett had been despatched to London at the start of the siege and wrote his account whilst the siege was in progress. The fact remains that every official document that came out of Londonderry during the siege was signed first by Walker as Governor. Gervais Squire the Mayor, testified that he administered the oath of fidelity to Dr Walker and Colonel Baker as Governors of Londonderry, and that Walker held precedence. Squire was accused of falsehoods, and this was the way Mackenzie got round it; there is even support from Walker's opponents. James II described him as a fierce minister of the Gospel '. . . of the true Cromwellian stamp'. He goes on to say that the citizens of Londonderry resolved to defy their king. They chose Baker and Walker as Governors. In *Light to the Blind* it is stated that there were two Governors at Londonderry, one Mr George Walker, a minister and the other Major Henry Baker. There is strong evidence therefore that Walker was a Governor, and we must give the last word to Dr Joseph Boyce, a Presbyterian minister, who praised Walker's role in the siege, saying that he gave 'eminent service to the interest of their Majesties and the Protestant religion'.

Baker and Walker therefore took over the defence of Londonderry, and were faced with a World War II situation. Fighting had already taken place, and the Catholics had swept all before them, and were now almost at the gates. Decisions had to be taken fast and things were happening very fast. The garrison needed to be reorganized, for it found itself almost totally denuded of officers, for most of them were escaping to Culmore, disappearing down the Foyle in boats, acting upon Lundy's advice. They were making their escape back to England.

The townsfolk were enraged when they learnt that their officers were running away and leaving them to their fate. They attacked them with such vigour that one Captain Bell was shot dead as he hurried into a boat and another officer was wounded. The fares back to England were expensive, and the Royal Navy led the way in charging what the market could bear. The Parliamentary Committee was later told by Colonel Chichester that Captain Cornwall, Commander of the *Swallow* frigate, when he returned to England, brought a great number of Protestant passengers aboard his ship and demanded £4 a head. Where the money was not to be had, he plundered them of their swords, watches, clothes or anything they had in a very barbarous manner. Nearly everyone knew everyone else within Derry's walls, and the garrison was quickly reorganized. Baker and Walker decided to have eight regiments, seven of foot and one of horse, each taking command of a regiment for himself, and then appointing six more colonels — Croften, Mitchelburne, Hamill, Murray, Parker and Whitney. The rank and file were divided into 117 companies, with sixty men to each company, producing a total fighting strength of over 7,000 men. Junior officers were appointed. *Londerias* says that 'the Colonels their subaltern officers chose'. According to Mackenzie the captains were elected by the men themselves, which

83

was a democratic arrangement that worked well enough for a citizen army. These arrangements were confirmed by George Holmes, who claimed to be the first in uniform to have revolted from King James and to have established opposition to Popery within the walls of Londonderry. He wrote from Strabane to his friend William Fleming of Conniston Hall when the siege was over, saying that 'we chose captains and completed regiments . . . All our officers fled away, so we made officers of those that did deserve to be officers. I was made captain'.

Each captain chose for himself under which Colonel his company would serve with the result that the regiments varied in strength. The final order of battle came out as fellows:–

> Baker's regiment 25 companies;
> Mitchelburne's 17;
> Walker's 15;
> Hamill's 14;
> Parker's and Whitney's 13 each;
> Crofton's 12;
> Murray's (the cavalry) 8.

There was eagerness to serve under Baker's banner and Walker too had plenty of support. The smallness of Murray's command can be explained by the lack of horses. Chaplains were appointed by the colonels; some chose Episcopalian clergymen and other dissenting ministers for this was a time when Church and Kirke joined together in opposition to the Catholics. In times of peace, the two Protestant churches disagreed, but in diversity they sympathized.

There were eighteen Episcopalian clergymen in Londonderry at the start of the siege according to Walker, and seven Nonconformist ministers, who looked after their flock very well. The Presbyterians in Londonderry felt that they were being patronized and Walker offended them in his published account by professing not to know the names of any of the seven, not even the name of the chaplain of his own regiment, John Mackenzie of Derryloran.

The heavy guns were drawn up — Roaring Meg and her sisters. *Londerias* said that:–

> Watson's made master of th' artillery
> Two hundred gunners and matrosses he
> James Murray was conductor of the train
> Our engineer was Adams of Strabane
> For Town-Major they chose Major Freemen.

A simple plan was adopted, the city, being divided into eight sectors and a regiment assigned to each; each company knowing their own bastion. The eight regimental adjutants were quartered together so that they could be found on all occasions. Each regiment's drummers were billeted in one house, so that on the least notice they repaired to the respective post of the company they belonged to. Upon the alarm being sounded, without any parading, all officers and private men came into their own ground and places, without the least disorder or confusion. Two regiments stood to each night, their adjutants remaining at the Main Guard until their regiments were relieved. There was curfew and a blackout; there was no drinking after eight o'clock at night; no candles were to be lit which might direct the enemy fire at the town in the night-time. The ammunition was removed from the main magazine, and lodged in four different places, in case of accidental fire or betrayal. Orders were issued to conserve powder and shot by avoiding unnecessary firing. A salmon and a half, two pounds of salt beef and four quarts of oatmeal were the rations for each private soldier. This allowance was sufficiently great to cast doubt upon Lundy's pessimistic estimates. Innkeepers were forbidden to charge more than a penny a quart for beer. The soldiers received no pay. As the merchants fled Londonderry, they left behind their stores, and they were gathered together into one place to prevent looting. All these arrangements were quickly completed:–

> Out of the broken regiments they chose
> The soldiers which the army did comprise.
> The Governors all matters soon dispose.

Baker and Walker acted effectively and they must be given credit for this; they set to rights the blunders of Lundy's incompetence. They reformed the broken regiments and made good Lundy's failure to draw up a plan of action against a siege. They had no choice but to act with all speed, for the Catholics, having gained much confidence at their success at the river fords, were approaching the city. The Jacobites were confident at their ability to reduce Londonderry, and the Irish army was accompanied by no less than King James himself.

There had been bitter arguments in Dublin whether King James should accompany the army north to join with the forces outside the town. The Catholics wanted to keep him in Dublin, and part of the reason for this, was that the Irish Parliament wanted his consent to a series of measures to stamp the Protestants even further into the mud. They realized that if the king were successful he would quickly lose interest in his Irish Kingdom and would concentrate upon English affairs. He would no longer be interested in righting Catholic wrongs in Ireland. Avaux, the French ambassador, only interested in his country's affairs, thought it unlikely that James would win back the throne. Avaux thought that the best plan was for Ireland to be severed from the English Crown, purged of its English colonists, reunited to the Catholic Church, placed under the protection of France, and for all intents and purposes to be made a province of that country. How long Williamite England would have tolerated this state of affairs is a matter for speculation. Tyrconnel supported Avaux so strongly that the French ambassador wrote appreciatively, if he were born a Frenchman he could not have supported France's ambitions more thoroughly. Tyrconnel was always avid to take fresh measures against

Irish Protestants. Avaux and the Irish regarded James as a tool to be manipulated in their own interests, but the king and his advisers regarded France as merely a tool to bring about their own desires. English and Scottish Jacobites had returned from exile in France to support their king, and for them Ireland was only a stepping stone to Great Britain. They had a leader in Melfort, Secretary of State, whom Avaux paid an unintended compliment when he said that Melfort was neither a good Irishman nor a good Frenchman. Melfort's task of persuasion was not difficult, for James too had his eyes fixed upon England. This meant travelling to Ulster as quickly as possible, so that Londonderry could be taken, and the city used as a stepping stone to Scotland. Here he would join Dundee's Highlanders. Tyrconnel had it that Avaux might not be able to take Londonderry so easily, and nobody thought that the city could hold out for more than a few days. To the military eye the defences seemed contemptible. The fortifications consisted of a simple wall overgrown with grass and weeds. There was no ditch, even before the gates. The drawbridge had long been neglected, and the chains were rusty. The parapets and towers were built after a fashion which as Macaulay said 'might well move disciples of Vauban to laughter'. The defences were on all sides surrounded by hills. Avaux was confident that a single battalion might take Londonderry in a day. It was argued to James that there was little glory to be obtained at the place. Even if the town surrendered there would be no triumph. There would be disgrace if the city put up a successful resistance.

It has been put forward that James made his way north for the simple reason that the city was on the point of surrender and that he was vain enough to want to be there when it did. James himself wrote in his memoirs that the journey to Derry might be hazardous, but that he was resolved to undertake it so that he would show faith in his generals. If Londonderry resisted, it would be imputed to him, and that his effort in going north would be seen as an effort to bring about a peaceful surrender. The Protestants of Londonderry were under the delusion that he had died at Brest and was not in Ireland at all. James was resolved to appear before the walls himself to disband any doubts in the citizens' minds that he was alive and determined to bring about surrender.

James was probably glad to escape from the clutches of the Irish Parliament in Dublin. To James the Parliament was a monster that had got out of hand in view of its demands. James never forgot that he was first and foremost King of England. He had burst out indignantly, when the Parliament demanded measures against the Protestants, that the Irish were heading for another 1641. The honest answer to this would have been "Yes!" If James remained in Dublin, it would have been scarcely impossible for him to withhold assent from any bill which the Irish Parliament presented. He would be forced to entrap and plunder innocent Protestant clergy and gentlemen by the hundreds. He would thus do irreparable damage to his cause in England. On the other hand, by moving north, he would be within a few hours' sail of Great Britain. In Scotland, his friends were supposed to be numerous. Once in England, assuming he won the Crown, he would be able to ignore the demands of the Irish Parliament.

James left Dublin for the North on 8th April, accompanied by Rosen and Avaux, who did not want to be left behind, despite his advice to the king. The journey was miserable, for the land had been laid waste by retreating Irish Protestant and Catholic robbers. General Pusignan wrote to Avaux that it was like travelling through the deserts of Arabia. The weather was very bad, although it was Springtime. The soldiers were continually drenched by showers of icy rain, and a freezing wind blew strongly from the north-west. No one felt more uncomfortable than Avaux. There was no accommodation to be found for him at Armagh. A brute of a billeting officer said that there was accommodation available for him in a filthy kitchen, full of soldiers smoking, drinking, talking, singing and in all making capital out of the question. Avaux pointed out that there were many suitable houses available and that he and his staff had been kept waiting in the rain for two hours. He was rudely told that he might remain in the rain and that there was no suitable accommodation for him. James was furious when he heard about the incident and at once broke the billeting officer. Avaux however pleaded for his reinstatement. However the lout treated them in the same way when they reached Omagh. The food was bad, and wheaten bread and wine were only available at the king's table. The food was carefully doled out to his favoured guests, whilst the others had to make do with horse corn and drink either water or bad beer made with oats instead of barley. It was flavoured with a nameless herb instead of hops.

There was a general irritable atmosphere and this was not helped by James's indifference. Avaux reported that the discontent as a result of these conditions was increased by James's insensibility; he seemed to be unaware that everyone around him was uncomfortable. There was always the risk of a raid by Protestants from Enniskillen and the French ambassador was not impressed by the men of the king's guard. The soldiers had not got sufficient weapons; in every company there were not four men that had swords; the old muskets and bad guns were unusable. They marched with powder, match or balls. The troops stole from their allies, and had little interest in protecting their king. Avaux was obliged to ask for a sentry to be posted at his billet whilst he was at Omagh. The soldiers were great thieves and his house had no door. Rosen, Maumont and Lery all had sentries, and Avaux stated that he never had a sentry, except when he arrived in Dublin. Avaux sighed for the comparative comfort of Dublin, and he was still trying to persuade James to turn back. He was convinced that the people of Londonderry would be seized by terror at the presence of the Catholic army and that the king's presence was unnecessary. He argued that if the citizens of Londonderry defended themselves, it would be a shameful retreat for the King of England. Melfort was all for the king going to the city, and Avaux feared that Melfort would win the argument about the king going to the town. Avaux knew that James had the tendency to give in to all of Melfort's ideas, and realized also that he could do little to persuade James otherwise.

Sunday 14th April came around, and news reached the Irish forces that the Protestants of Londonderry were massing to defend the fords of Mourne and the Finn; also they had word that Cunningham's fleet was lying in Lough Foyle. James lost his nerve and Avaux was summoned three times into the king's presence and was informed of the Protestant moves. He warmly approved of the decision to retreat south at once. At Charlemont, James heard about the Catholic victories of the river fords. There was also an unfounded rumour that the English fleet was not in Lough Foyle. James decided to make haste to Londonderry, whilst Avaux continued his usual policy of trying to persuade him otherwise. Avaux was of the opinion that the Protestants would not surrender to him merely because he was the king. They would not surrender through fear either, because they could see James in person with so few troops. This would only encourage them to hold out, and there would be much vexation within Catholic ranks if the Protestants successfully held out. There was always the choice, however, that the Protestants would believe that the Catholic forces were only part of the besieging army.

Avaux's arguments still made no impression upon James. Rosen had ridden forward to take command of the Catholic army and had distinguished himself in the fighting at Lifford. He had now passed Strabane and was reporting back that the people of Derry were negotiating for surrender. The appearance of James outside the walls would help matters, he said. James therefore rode on to Londonderry, whilst Avaux returned to Dublin where he would have the opportunity of telling the king that his advice was right.

Chapter 15

James II at Londonderry

George Walker knew that a considerable mood of fear was present in Londonderry, in view of the citizens' decision to hold out in the face of overwhelming odds. News of the approaching Catholic army caused some confusion amongst Protestant ranks. Many people were fleeing the city, and the garrison was thought not to be up to the assault that would take place. The English had left, having no confidence in Londonderry's ability to hold out. There were few horses to sally with and there was no forage. There were no engineers to instruct them in the defence. There was not as much as a hand grenade to combat the enemy; nor was there a gun well-mounted in the whole of the town. The Catholics were numerous and powerful. The Protestants thought that they were in as great a danger as the Israelites at the Red Sea. Like the Israelites the Protestants trusted in God, and they believed that God had chosen them for the defence of their city.

Lundy had told Cunningham that the Catholics were approaching Londonderry 25,000 strong. James was marching north to the city, it was said, with an impressive train of artillery. If the forces Richard Hamilton had brought from Coleraine and Pusignan from Charlemont are counted, then 25,000 men for the Catholic army would not be far off Lundy's estimate. Ten regiments of cavalry and twenty-five of infantry, with the normal strength of 600 men to a regiment, would also come close to Lundy's figure, giving the Irish army an impressive strength outside the city. However by no means all the regiments were up to strength and at least five of them had to be temporarily merged to produce between them just two battalions. The thirty-five regiments were not however present at Londonderry all at the same time. The army's lines of communications had to be considered against the threat Enniskillen posed. The troops were seldom paid and hundreds of men were always absent from their posts, out ravaging the countryside for food. In his *True Account* Joseph Bennett, a Derry Protestant, said that in those early days the Catholics had 7,000 men on the left bank of the Foyle and another 3,000 across the river on the Waterside. Bennett had found himself in the Catholic ranks for a while at the start of the siege. The Duke of Berwick said that the besieging army was 10,000 strong.

From time to time, reinforcements were sent up from the South, but these barely made up for the toll taken on the army by sickness, desertion and battle

89

casualties. Londonderry soon became a mincing machine for the Catholic forces. Walker said that the two opposing armies were about equal in strength. The Catholics were at an advantage in cavalry and dragoons; they had more of them and were better equipped. Their commanders were more experienced and they had plenty of fodder for their horses. However cavalry was very seldom used in besieging a walled town. The Catholic infantry were not very well equipped and were so short of weapons that one regiment arrived on the field with only seven muskets to be shared amongst 600 men.

Most of the Catholic soldiers before Londonderry were only armed with pointed sticks, without iron tips. Those who did possess muskets had little idea of how to use them. The matchlock was still the standard weapon, despite the fact that the flintlock was taking its place. The matchlock was not an easy weapon to handle, despite its ingenious lock, but it made a great improvement over the primitive handguns that had preceded it. However the matchlock was still slow and clumsy. The powder had to be ignited by a glowing lump of match or tow, so that it was a dangerous weapon if handled anywhere near gunpowder, and it was almost useless in wind and rain. It required considerable skill to make the matchlock fire at all, and this could be done with little accuracy. When William's General Schomberg, ordered practise for his troops that faced the Catholics at the Battle of the Boyne a year later, it was observed that few had any skill in using them. This must have been equally true of the Protestants, for a Jacobite writer noted that the Irish soldiers trembled, making a good aim difficult. A matchlock in very good condition was hard to handle, and a badly maintained matchlock was impossible.

Rosen complained about the inefficient armaments sent to him and James, inspecting regiments on his way to Londonderry, was surprised to find the muskets in such a bad condition, so that not one hundred of them were fit for service. Richard Hamilton's army at Strabane was no better off for want of arms and ammunition. Few of the Catholic infantrymen had any idea of how to look after their weapons. Avaux noted that good muskets had been lost by neglect or were broken through the carelessness of the men and their officers. He warned James that if he were to send over 50,000 new muskets, more than 40,000 would be of any use within six months. It was also a fact that nearly all the gunsmiths in Ireland were Protestants, who did not go to much trouble in servicing the weapons of the Catholic army. When James returned to Dublin, he found that the Protestant gunsmiths had not been over enthusiastic about repairing weapons. Tyrconnel complained of sabotage, saying that the armourers did more damage than usefulness to the muskets in the Catholic arsenal.

The prime requisite in besieging a walled town however was not muskets but artillery. One hundred years earlier, William Bourne in a treatise had explained how to go about battering walls. He said that the fire of six cannon had to be concentrate upon one spot, thus making a breach. Scaling the walls became practicable. Although the Irish had a contingent of experienced French artillerymen under command of de Pointis, they do not seem to have been aware of this rule, for their cannon were ineffective. The cannon was discharged over the walls, amongst the houses and at sallying parties. The artillery of the Catholics was quite unsuitable for a siege.

Richard Hamilton, in marching up to Londonderry from Strabane, was anxious to hide his army, lest the Protestants might see its weakness and continue in their rebellion against James. According to Walker the Catholics arrived outside the city with one large and two small mortars and twelve field guns. There were not in the Catholic camp more than eight cannon, two of which were pounders. A contemporary writer, Macpherson, said that James sent to Derry two cannon, one great mortar to breach the walls in accordance with the ideas of William Bourne. The mortar was useless because of its high trajectory, although it was very useful for firing missiles over the walls and dropping them on the houses within. An explosive bomb was fired, a round missile described by an early writer as a hollow shot of cast iron, stuffed with fireworks or wild fire.

On the high ground on the opposite side of the Foyle, the mortars could be used with great effect. A battery of these was established in an orchard which belonged to a man called Stronge, a Protestant colonist. The bombs, according to Walker, weighed over 270lbs apiece and contained several pounds of powder in the shell. The streets were ploughed up by the bombs, and broke down the houses, so that no one could walk in the streets or stay indoors. All had to flock to the walls and the remotest parts of the town. Many of the sick were killed because they could not leave their houses. Day and by night, Londonderry was bombarded, and the effect of this must have been like the Blitz in London during 1940 and 1941. Death met the citizens of Londonderry at every corner and in their houses they were totally insecure. They could not rest in bed without thinking about the siege.

Without a train of artillery to batter down the walls, this meant that the Catholics had to starve the city into surrender. The people of Londonderry actively tried to let civilians and others leave the town, thus reducing the demand on the garrison's food supply. Walker says that the Catholics promised to assist and harbour all those Protestants who left Londonderry. 10,000 noncombatants left the city upon hearing the Irish declaration, and many eventually grew weary of remaining in the city. At the start of the siege, the population of Londonderry was 30,000, and this was cut by a third by desertions. Richard Hamilton was responsible for this policy, perhaps from motives of humanity or perhaps because he wanted to hear useful information from the deserters. Hamilton was convinced his policy was correct and he ignored orders from James that no more Protestants should be coaxed to leave the city. Rosen, returning from Dublin to take charge of the siege for the second time, halted the flood of refugees. He drove into Derry a number of useless mouths from the surrounding countryside. His barbaric methods were eventually to prove more than James and his commanders could tolerate.

There was a considerable death rate in Londonderry amongst the old, the young and the weak, which enabled the garrison to hold out that much longer. The number of dead probably ran into several thousands. George Holmes wrote that at least 15,000 died as result of the privations. There were great fevers amongst the garrison and all the children died, and whole families perished. People were 'swept away' daily in large numbers by a great fever, says another contemporary account. People died that fast that there was no room to bury them, and even the gardens were filled up with the dead. Some were even thrown into cellars. Thus it was the great privations, carrying off large numbers and Hamilton's policy of letting Protestants leave the city, that helped Londonderry hold out. None of these facts could be known to the garrison at the start of the siege, as they awaited the arrival of what they understood to be a well-organized and large Catholic army. This army had already routed them twice with remarkable ease.

The Catholic victories of Dromore and the river fords had been mainly won by the cavalry. The Protestants were soon to find out that the Irish infantry were far inferior to the Catholic cavalry. The Catholics were wanting in training and discipline. The French officers were competent enough, but they had to act through interpreters in order to command the Irish. The transmission of orders in heated moments was rather difficult. The French found that the Irish were a heavy and laborious people. John Stevens, an English officer, who served with the Jacobite army in Ireland, said that the Catholic rank and file would follow none but their own leaders.

Many of the Irish commanders were as ignorant of discipline as their troops. The Irish had little liking for their French allies, and during lulls in the siege, they freely expressed their hatred of them to the Protestants who were manning the walls. They expressed 'great prejudice and hatred of the French, cursing them'. James nor Rosen did not seem to understand that the Catholics, so poorly armed, poorly led and so poorly paid, could possibly fight with any valour. James exclaimed that if he had Englishmen in his army, he would have been able to capture Londonderry 'stone by stone'. Rosen reported to Louvois, the French Minister of War, that the Irish soldiers generally were a bunch of undisciplined rabble. Irish soldiers were to prove themselves later in the service of France, if properly led and disciplined, as effective troops with valour and honour, and a match for the best troops in Europe.

There was one other circumstance that told in favour of the besieged, though this was not realized immediately. This point is well made by Sean O'Faolin in his description of Mountjoy's army at the siege of Kinsale nearly ninety years before. He said that the idea of a siege was that the besieged were caught like rats in a trap and that their position was desperate. The attackers were worse off, especially in a Winter campaign. They are exposed to bad weather, so that their trenches were filled with water. They are therefore miserable all the time and they die of disease. On the other hand the besieged lived in comfortable houses and all they had to do was to build up breaches made by cannon. They have to sally forth to combat the besiegers. If a besieged town had plenty of food, it can hold out for some time, given good spirits on behalf of the besieged. The siege of Londonderry was, unlike the Kinsale siege, not a Winter campaign. The weather in the Spring and Summer of 1689 was exceptionally cold and wet. The citizens of Londonderry however would not have regarded themselves as living in comfortable houses, for there was much overcrowding. They were subjected to constant bombardment by the mortars. Otherwise what was true of Kinsale in 1601 was true of Londonderry in 1689, when the besiegers had to live in worse conditions than the besieged. On the Catholic side most of the soldiers had to live in tents and a great number of them had to survive in cold damp huts whose walls were made of sods of turf, dugouts sunk four or five feet below ground level. These sheltered them from Protestant shot, says Ash, and in such conditions, disease must have set in.

At the beginning of the siege, the Protestants were not aware of the deficiencies in the Catholic army and the difficulties which it must inevitably have faced in laying siege to the city. The only thing the Protestants were aware of, according to Walker, was their own fighting strength, 7,020 men any 341 officers. Walker, responsible for doling out the rations, was well placed to know the position; his figures are in line with other contemporary estimates. Protestants were as poorly disciplined as Catholics, with the exception of Mountjoy's regiment of 300 men. Their lack of training showed when they met the Catholics at the battle of the river fords. Now fighting from behind walls, they might promise to fare better, if they could keep their nerve and shoot straight.

Of the 341 officers, a few had experience, such as Mitchelburne, but the great majority were amateurs. The titles of colonel, mayor and captain were freely bestowed and used, but this did not indicate that the bearers had any military experience. The garrison's weapons included swords, muskets, pikes and even on occasion, stones and scythes. The scythe was an extremely effective weapon for it could inflict horrible injuries. The men who used it in battle were called 'shavers' and at Preston Pains, over half a century later, the Macgregor clansmen were able to cut heads, legs off horses and cut men's bodies into pieces.

The Londonderry men had also a few long duck guns, and sometimes they were able to capture from the Catholics firelocks, muskets, saddles, bridles and entrenching tools. There was no shortage of powder and shot from the outset, according to Ash. According to George Holmes, cannon bullets flew as fast as one could count them, and as soon as enemy cannonballs landed, they were sent back post-paid.

A body of yeoman cavalry were there at the start of the siege under the leadership of Adam Murray, who fought with great skill and courage in several sorties. Soon forage ran short, and by the end of the siege horses were being used as meat. During the siege there was no forage for the horses, so the Protestants were forced to let them out and the enemy captured many. The rest of them died of hunger.

Before the opening of hostilities there was a ritual of negotiations that took place between Protestants and Catholics. Whilst James was still hurrying to catch up with his army, Richard Hamilton had taken the first steps. Hamilton made generous promises and violent threats. He said that 'here is your king, that resolves to perform all the conditions you can desire'. If the men of Londonderry surrendered they would enjoy generous terms. They would be 'Favourites and Finishers of this difficult Siege and insure reduction of Ireland'. They might expect as their reward all the lands of the absentees and other such persons who would be disinherited. All their existing lands would be confirmed to them by Act of Parliament. The Protestants were promised that they would be allowed to serve with James in Scotland and England, where thousands of both nations were there to receive them and join the Jacobite cause. The Protestants were promised to be sharers in the forfeited lands. They were informed that Duke Gordon was now in possession of Edinburgh Castle for the king; Dundee was in arms and all James's friends were there to receive him.

If the Protestants continued to resist, then there would be terrible consequences. Their ruin would be inevitable, and if the Protestants still proved to be obstinate, no quarter would be given to man, woman or child. Once the Catholic cannon had breached the walls and the city taken by storm, then all the people of Derry would implore pity from James. The Catholic army would be merciless. Plunket, an Irish Jacobite writer, was however highly critical of the generous terms that the Catholics offered to the Protestants, when inducing them to surrender. He said that James, despite previous experience, would not be more cautious in dealing with Protestants; he was over indulgent towards them. As Lundy was presiding over the last session of his Council, Hamilton's terms arrived at the city. The garrison asked for time to consider, and asked that the Catholic army should keep its distance, which Walker put at four miles, two and a half according to another source, and not nearer than Saint Johnston according to the Duke of Berwick. The garrison thought that Berwick had agreed to this, as indeed he may have done, for as we have seen he was anxious to keep his army out of sight lest the Protestants discover its weakness. Rosen now arrived to take over command, and thought that the presence of the Catholic army would make the Protestants surrender.

On 18th April, at ten o'clock in the morning, James and Rosen led their troops, colours flying, up towards Bishop's Gate, a moment recorded in the Protestant folk song 'Derry's Walls':–

> When James and all his rebel band
> Came up to Bishop's Gate,
> They bravely stood before the walls,
> And forced him to retreat.

The Protestants were amazed, and to James's astonishment and terror, there thundered from the ramparts a great discharge of cannon and musquetry, which continued for most of the day. At the same time, from the walls, came the cry of "No Surrender!" — the battle cry of Ulster Protestants throughout the ages.

Captain Troy was killed at the king's side, and at this a large number of

Catholics took to their heels, for they could not be kept in order by their officers. James was surprised by the reaction of his army and also by the reaction of the besieged, for he had heard other stories about their expected behaviour. The king remained sitting upon his horse for the rest of the day. He was bombarded with cannon of 14, 16 and 22 pounds weight. He himself was just out of range of the cannonade from the walls; he ate nothing, and as evening approached, he retired to Saint Johnston to await his artillery and other necessities for a siege. He continued to persuade the citizens to surrender, and for this, the prospects seemed good. Baker and Walker were in the process of taking over as Governors, but they did not seem too resolved upon resistance. They had tried to get Lundy to resume his office, and when he refused, they connived at his escape. They now sent an apology to James for the firing from the walls, which they blamed upon the rabble who, having been drunk, fired the cannon without authority from the town. They said that the better sort of people in the town were intent upon surrender and did all they could to persuade the common sort to do so.

There was no trigger-happy mob within Londonderry inflamed by drink, but rather a garrison inflamed by rumours of treachery. They became alarmed when they saw soldiers approach in breach of Hamilton's promises. Hamilton had said that he would not come within four miles of the walls, and the people imagined that they had been betrayed. They thought that it was in keeping for them to fire their guns at the Catholics. Rosen was blamed for this incident by Berwick, for James, he said, had been aware of Hamilton's promise to the Protestants. James accepted the garrison's apologies, and according to George Holmes, he sent a letter written by himself, sealed with his own seal, to induce the citizens of Londonderry to surrender, but saying that they could have their own conditions. The Earl of Abercorn bore the letter. He had been sent not to offer the garrison their own terms, as Holmes thought, but to invite them to send twenty representatives under safe conduct to St Johnston to discuss surrender. The Duke was kept outside the gates, and the people on the walls could hear him shouting that a capitulation had better take place. At this some of the less resolute Protestants hurried off to St Johnston to make their submission and receive protection. The members of the new Council, which had replaced Lundy's regiment, were as faint-hearted as he was. They at once set about organizing twenty representatives to be sent to James to attempt a surrender. Adam Murray refused an invitation to be one of the number, and he left the meeting to take up his post at the walls, and no doubt to warn the citizens of what the Council was planning. When the delegation left the town, the people on the walls said that if the delegation surrendered to James, they would be a traitor to the Protestant religion and to King William.

With the fate of Captain Bell in mind, no one was willing to risk the people's wrath. From this moment thoughts of surrender were put aside. Instead a reply, believed to have been drafted by a Captain Maltis, was sent to Melfort at St Johnston. It said that the Protestants would maintain their position, and that God would defend them against Popery. They said that King William was just as capable of rewarding them as King James, and that an English Parliament would be just as capable of looking after their interests as an Irish one. They would be just as capable of keeping their lands under William than under James. Londonderry proclaimed its defiance with these words, and they said that if James's trumpeter would again come to the walls, he would be fired upon.

James now had a siege on his hands, and he realised that he could do little if he hung around the city. He therefore handed over command of the army to the French general, Maumont, with Pusignan, Hamilton and Berwick as his subordinates. James, accompanied by Rosen and Melfort returned to Dublin, where he could not have been looking forward to seeing Avaux, who said that everything had happened at Londonderry, as he had foretold. James had spent two days before Londonderry and had four times summoned the city to surrender, but in vain. He had now been obliged to return to Dublin, a place that he should never have left, if he had listened to the French ambassador. Avaux said that the king was quite mortified by the events which had taken place at the city.

Chapter 16

Blackmail Threats

James left it up to his local commanders whether they should attack or blockade Londonderry. According to Berwick the first priority was to establish a blockade while they waited for supplies which they needed in order to effect a siege. There was little else they could do until the heavy artillery train came up from Dublin. However, some of the Jacobite leaders saw that time was not on their side, and that every day lost at Londonderry kept them away from joining Dundee in Scotland. Also it meant that William would be able to gain time, for he was planning to send a fleet to the city stronger than Cunningham's. The Catholics wanted to besiege Derry with their whole army and then drive on to Scotland. Others saw the position at Londonderry as an opportunity to give their unseasoned troops experience in battle, and they persuaded James to take a middle of the road stance, for they wanted him to conduct a slow and regular siege, which would teach the men to be better soldiers. James lost his opportunity in not sending reinforcements to Dundee and so to have changed the course of the conflict.

Macaulay said that Maumont, now in command at Londonderry, had much to his credit. According to a contemporary polemic, Maumont and Rosen were very cruel men, and that they had committed atrocities on the Continent. If this was true the Protestants of Londonderry were soon to avenge the Huguenots of Languedoc. Maumont ringed Londonderry with sixteen infantry regiments, strung out in a semicircle, a position that had been taken up by Rosen. Each end of the arc rested on the River Foyle, one above Londonderry and the other below, so that on the landward side the city was surrounded by Catholics. This provided a formidable sight to the garrison, so unused to warfare. On the opposite bank of the Foyle, Maumont established a position under command of Lord Bellow and Lord Louth, a command based in Stronge's Orchard, from where the Catholics bombarded the town. To prevent help reaching the garrison through County Londonderry — and further downstream — Sir Michael Creagh was posted with a detachment at a point where the boom was later placed over the river.

The fort of Culmore was captured on 23rd April. It was small and not very well built, but it commanded the narrow channel, where the river enters the lough. In Catholic hands, the capture of Culmore should have made it virtually

97

impossible for the English, to have relieved Londonderry by sea. Lundy had given the order that Culmore was to be evacuated, but it was later reoccupied by a larger garrison, including 300 men from the city, under command of William Adaire of Ballymena. All its guns had been taken to Londonderry, except for one iron gun and four small pieces of artillery. Adaire surrendered the fort without firing a shot when troops arrived in the area, although according to Berwick, they 'had not the means of taking it'.

Rumours of treachery were soon flying about, and Joseph Bennett claimed that James had bribed the garrison's commanders. 'A Full Relation of the Surrendering of Kulmore' says that 'the persuasion of a small spill of French gold (the true way of French courage in taking towns)' was how the surrender was effected. Ash blamed Adaire and his brother, together with 'Galbraith the attorney' saying that within a fortnight after the siege began, 'sold Culmore to the enemy for a considerable sum of money'. However Ash admits that he did not know if there was much truth in the story, but it was said that one of the Adaires had lost his reason, giving the explanation that this was how God was punishing him for conniving with the French.

The Adaire that went mad had been probably driven so by the way which the terms to the Culmore garrison had been broken. The Culmore garrison had been guaranteed a full pardon and a return to their homes with all their possessions, including their swords; and the officers were to remain in possession of their horses and pistols, with one gun each for sporting purposes. By the order of Colonel Charles Moor, Governor of Coleraine — to which town they wanted to go — they were not only disarmed but stripped to their shirts, their money taken from them and the Culmore garrison sent out begging. They complained to Richard Hamilton and he said that if the perpetrators could be shown to be soldiers, they would be punished. He said that he could do nothing about the behaviour of the rabble. The loss of Culmore did not become known in Londonderry for some weeks, and the garrison only learnt of it from letters taken from soldiers that were killed in action.

The Protestants of Londonderry had chalked up a victory, their first in an engagement at Pennyburn; this happened two days before the Culmore garrison surrendered. The little Pennyburn river runs into the Foyle about a mile below Londonderry's walls. In those days there was a village of the same name and a water mill. Maumont, on the night of 20th April — having established his headquarters three miles away — ordered Pennyburn to be occupied by a force of infantry under command of Colonel John Hamilton, another of the Hamilton brood. Next morning Hamilton's men 'could be seen from Londonderry, moving up to the village. Adam Murray at once decided to attack with his yeomanry. Most of the horses in the city were out grazing, and there was a shortage of forage'. He could only muster a hundred troopers, half of which he led himself, and the rest being led by Major Nathaniel Bull. The operation was ordered in a very casual fashion. The men sallied out not in a very commendable fashion. Murray had also ordered out 500 musketeers who took up their position on the high ground that overlooked Pennyburn. An urgent appeal was sent to Hamilton for reinforcements and the Commander in Chief responded in person. Hamilton was short of horses himself, after most of his mounted men were out foraging, so he took with him the only cavalry available, a troop of forty men. He picked up a troop of dragoons on the way, and headed at full gallop towards Pennyburn. He at once clashed with the Protestants. Maumont was killed, but from the outset Murray's men were forced to retreat towards Londonderry, chased by the Irish cavalry, the leader of which was praised by Mackenzie. The leader in all probability was the Duke of Berwick.

The Reverend George Walker now appeared upon the scene. As he saw Murray's force being driven back towards Londonderry, he mounted one of the horses and made them rally, to relieve Murray, whom he saw was surrounded by the Catholics. Murray was fighting with great courage, but it was a matter of opinion whether Murray or Walker was performing best. According to Walker's account, he praised his own performance on the field, and self-praise was a habit of the Reverend.

As the Catholic cavalry rode in pursuit of Murray, they suffered a lot from gunfire from the Protestant muskets hiding behind hedges. They also came under gunfire from the walls, and at this they turned back to Pennyburn. For a second time they came under the fire of the Protestant musketeers, and now they were almost wiped out. Berwick said that of those that escaped death, not a man nor a horse was left wounded.

Reports of the Pennyburn skirmish reached Dublin and they had become distorted; it was said that the Londonderry garrison had killed 4 or 5,000 of the Catholic soldiers. *Londerias* only claims half that number, for:–

Two thousand slain the riverside they filled,
And many officers of note were killed.

Both of these figures are highly exaggerated, but the Duke of Berwick's estimate is too low, for he gave his own side's losses at two officers and six other ranks killed. Walker says that the Catholics killed 'above 200 of the enemy soldiers'. Mackenzie agrees, saying that he was not sure about the number dead, but he put this at 200. Joseph Bennett, temporarily a prisoner in the Catholic camp, put the total Irish dead at about sixty. The estimates were indeed wild, but there was no doubt that in the Catholic camp, Maumont had been killed, although there was some argument as to the manner of his death. It was rumoured that Adam Murray had killed him in hand-to-hand combat in an Homeric fashion. Avaux however reported that he had been killed by a musket shot. Macaulay doubts the story that Maumont was killed by Murray, but Mackenzie believed it and Mitchelburne, a lover of self-praise like Walker, wrote in his play that Murray excelled up the field of battle and that he slew Maumont. Ash mentions nothing about a combat between Maumont and Murray, and Walker is silent about it, but Walker was mainly interested in his own performance and not that of others.

Aicken, who was in Londonderry at the time, has a long passage about what happened between Murray and Maumont:–

> The Strand thus clear'd, Murray and Maumont meet,
> Who with dire threatenings one another greet;
> For they oft parted in the bloody rout.
> First they discharged their pistols on the spot,
> In which first firing Murray's horse was shot;
> Yet the brave heart ne'er felt the deadly wound
> But wheel'd and pranced upon the bloody ground!
> Redoubled blows they gave with sword in hand,
> Which the strong armour scarcely would withstand.
> They thunder like the Cyclops at the forge,
> When the metal on the anvil urge.
> At last their swords in sev'ral pieces flew,
> Then with their rapiers they the fight renew;
> The brave Maumont began to falsify
> And thought the day his own immediately:
> He wheel'd his horse, which then began to spurn,
> But noble Murray made a quick return,
> For under hear'd arm his sword he thrust,
> Till at his neck the purple gave out burst.
> His fleeing soul with the free blood expir'd,
> And our great hero to the foot retir'd.

The sword with which Murray killed Maumont — supposing that he did so — is still preserved and his great-grandson was much elated at this first skirmish at Pennyburn. This is depicted in *Ireland Preserved*, and Mitchelburne, who calls himself Granado in the play, congratulates Monrath, who in real life was Murray, and mentions that the success at Pennyburn will much enliven his men. Moreover it was said that the Protestants had captured a piebald horse at Pennyburn and that Saint Columba had prophesied the end of Catholic hopes.

Murray's losses had been slight, but his force had not escaped without casualty, for Cornet Brown was slain; Macphetrix died upon 'the purple plain'; Lieutenant MacKay was slain, and M'Cleland's son was wounded with a shot.

The slain were buried with much ceremony, ceremonies which later had to be foregone as the number of dead mounted. The Catholics quickly reinforced Pennyburn, but four days later Murray again sallied out to dislodge them. To dislodge the Catholics from Pennyburn was not as easy as the poem *Londerias* claimed.

The fight went on all day, having started at nine o'clock in the morning. Each side travelled too far in pursuit and had to turn back in flight. According to Mackenzie, the Protestants pursued the Catholics as far as Pennyburn Mill. The commanding officer of the Coleraine regiment, Colonel Parker, was sent with a rearguard to protect Murray's men as they returned to the city. Murray

100

succeeded in getting his men safely back to Londonderry.

The spectators on the wall had a grandstand view of events. Colonel Parker appeared so slow and negligent in the discharge of his duty as to expose the returning Protestants to great danger. He was threatened with a court martial and prudently left Londonderry that night and joined the Catholics. Captain Lane took over command of the Coleraine regiment, having been promoted to Colonel's rank.

Despite the small size of the skirmishes at Pennyburn, these initial victories were good for the garrison's morale. The men of Londonderry at once forgot about the defeats at Dromore and the river fords. At Pennyburn, man for man, they had been a match for the Catholics. The Protestants were soon telling the Catholics that they had no need to make a breach in the wall with cannon, because they always kept the gates open and that the passage through the gates was wider than any breach they could make. Maumont had been killed after having been Commander in Chief for two days.

In the second battle 'Pontee' and Berwick had been wounded and General Pusignan, who had been senior general upon Maumont's death, had received a mortal wound. The wound could have been seen to by any reasonably skilled surgeon, but none was available, and when one did arrive from Dublin, it was only to find that the funeral had taken place. Pusignan died complaining about the ignorance which was then prevalent in his days. Avaux reported to Louvois that Pusignan had not only died of his wounds but from the horrors of realizing that there was no help available. With Pusignan's death, command of the Catholic army went to Richard Hamilton, whom Macaulay describes as a fine gentleman and a brave officer, but that he was not a great general and that he had never in his life seen a siege. However none of the Protestants had seen a siege either. From France, Louvois wrote to Avaux that the French must take better care of their officers, and not lose them so easily. James had thought about this also, and he wrote to Hamilton that the generals were not to expose themselves and only to do so when Hamilton thought necessary. Plunket was annoyed that the rabble of Londonderry should kill a French general, and he commented that it was a misfortune to see French blood taken by such rascals. He also said that these were the first sacrifices on the French side as a result of the siege.

Hamilton was now no more than six battalions at Londonderry, with none up to its full strength of 600 men. He said that of every ten men not one had a weapon fit to shoot, and that he had need of urgent reinforcements of men, artillery and all other equipment needed to conduct a siege.

The people of Londonderry were also awaiting the horrors of the siege. The Catholics, on the first day of the Pennyburn siege, sited a demi-culverin in Stronge's Orchard, facing Shipquay Gate. They opened fire upon the houses of the town, doing some damage to the market house. The ancient guns on the bastion replied to some effect, killing Lieutenants Fitzpatrick and Con O'Neill, two sergeants, several soldiers and two friars. Walker said that it was to the grief of the citizens that the blood of these two friars were shed. Some days later the demi-culverin in the orchard was reinforced by mortars, whose high trajectory made them much more effective than the ordinary cannon. The bombs from the smaller mortars were quite harmless, all of them falling in the streets, except one which killed an old lady in a garret.

Soon much bigger bombs were flying through the air from the other side of the River Foyle, and there were some narrow escapes. One bomb fell into a house while several officers were at dinner; it fell upon the back of the room they were in, but it did not harm them. The bomb made its way into a lower room, killing the landlord. He said that he was in the next room one night at his supper when seven men were thrown out of the third room next to the room he was in, killing many and injuring others.

The garrison took protective measures, erecting blinds to shield the men posted on the walls. They pulled up the pavements to prevent stones being flung about by the explosives. On the night of 26th April, the bombs played wildly upon the city, with little intermission between sunset and sunrise. The 26th was a night of great suffering and terror prevailed everywhere, except in the hearts of the Londonderry heroes under arms. The shrieks of women and children mingled with the crash of houses felled by the bombs.

At about this time, Richard Hamilton conceived of an idea how to blackmail Adam Murray's eighty-year-old father; Hamilton had correctly identified Murray as a key figure in the defence. When Adam went for a soldier, the old man remained peacefully on his estate in Faughanvale, but he was now arrested and brought to Hamilton's headquarters. Hamilton ordered him to go to Londonderry and persuade Murray to surrender the town. If Murray refused to surrender then his father would be hanged. Old Murray told Hamilton that he would be going on a purposeless mission, for his son would never agree to surrender the town to James. When Old Murray met his son, he asked Adam to place his hand on a Bible, which he had brought with him, and urged Adam to swear:–

> Never to yield unto a Popish power,
> Our holy faith and loyalty enjoin.
> A strict abhorrence of a Popish reign.

Murray then returned to Catholic headquarters, presenting himself to be hanged but Hamilton was so moved by the old man that he escorted him safely back to his farm at Ling, where he allowed him to remain under protection for the remainder of the siege.

The action now shifted to the south of the city, to the high ground about 500 yards from Bishop's Gate. There was a ridge which was known as Windmill Hill, and which must also have been the sight of the town gibbet:–

> Near Bishop's Gate the fatal windmills lie,
> Where cattle feed and criminals do die.

The Protestants had stationed an outpost at the windmill; they had only a few guns and their long-barrelled flintlock fowling pieces. They had been making such a nuisance of themselves that Hamilton decided to dislodge them. He thought that Windmill Hill would make a good site for the heavy siege artillery, which was now said to be on its way up from Dublin.

Brigadier Ramsay of Pennyburn now decided to launch an attack against the Windmill Hill outpost on 5th May. This brigade was 3,000 strong and it was a surprise attack on Windmill Hill. He quickly drove off the Protestant pickets and by dawn he was consolidating his hold on the ridge by converting some ditches into a system of trenches which ran from the bog that covered his left flank to the river on his right.

The Protestants quickly launched a counterattack, for Ramsay was seen to be placing a battery on Windmill Hill. The besieged feared that the battery might incommode that part of the town nearest to it. An assault force was gathered by choosing ten men from each of the 117 companies. This was not enough for some impetuous spirits, who joined the sortie of their own accord. Mackenzie said that Governor Baker and other officers were about detaching ten out of every company to attack them, but the men were impatient and went on the attack of their own accord. Walker, with his usual tendency to self-praise, gives himself a leading part.

Walker drew a detachment out of each company of ten men and, after putting them into the best order their impatience could allow, 'he sallied out at the head of them at Ferry Key Gate at four o'clock in the morning'. Mackenzie says that this was invention, for if Walker had have done as he said it was not only with all imaginable silence but with so wonderful scenery too as to be neither seen nor heard by any of those that are said to follow him'. Walker was not mentioned among the eight or nine officers whom *Londerias* singles out for praise for their behaviour in this engagement. On the other hand it is not likely that Walker would have made a claim he could not later support.

Ash says that it was Baker and Walker jointly who ordered the sortie, but whoever commanded it, the result was a triumph, a sharp action decided by hand-to-hand fighting. According to Walker, one section of the sallying party beat the Catholic dragoons from the hedges whilst the other possessed their trenches. Although the Catholics had a considerable detachment, the fighting was soon over. The Catholics fled and left the Protestants the ground they contended for. They left some booty, besides their dead, and it was all over by noon.

The number of enemy dead was put by Walker at 200; the Irish sustained 500 wounded of whom 300 died within a few days, which revealed the poor state of medicine in the Catholic ranks. Protestant losses had been light, just three men killed and twenty wounded. They had captured five pairs of colours, and two of these were hung in the Cathedral to make the victory. The flagpoles remain today, although the fabric has rotted, but it has been replaced several times. Later on in the day, the Protestants invited the Catholics to come and bury their dead, which they did so very negligently, hardly covering their bodies with earth.

The Catholic casualties at Windmill Hill, as at Pennyburn, included prized

103

comrades, whose loss could not be afforded; chief amongst these was Ramsay himself, who was shot dead while he attempted to rally his men. Ash says that he was much lamented by all who knew him, for he was reckoned to be the best soldier in the Catholic side after Richard Hamilton. Mitchelburne had served under Ramsay in happier days ten years before, and gave his old commander a military funeral at the Long Tower. A velvet pall covered the coffin, on which lay the dead brigadier's sword, scarf and stick. Another host of officers, including Captains Fleming, Fox and Barnwell were also killed. The Protestants had taken a number of prisoners at the windmill, amongst them Sir Garrett Aylmer, Lieutenant Colonel William Talbot, one of Tyrconnel's kinsmen, and Viscount Netterville. The prisoners are depicted as arriving at Londonderry, in *Ireland Preserved*. Mitchelburne boasts to Baker of his feats at Windmill Hill, when where according to the stage directions, there is a great shout within, saying that a way should be made for Lord Netterville. His lordship enters with two soldiers supporting him, and with three of his fingers cut off and a wound on his face. Lord Netterville appears as a fat man and sits down in a chair. Baker, not having heard the shout within, asks Lord Netterville who he is, and Netterville tells him who he is and what had happened to him. "What?" cries Baker in surprise. "My Lord Netterville?"

Netterville replies that he is seventy years of age, that he had to turn soldier, and that his spirits were low. He requested that he should be able to lie down. Baker cried that Netterville should have a surgeon immediately, for his lordship was fainting, and that he should have a glass of sack at once. The sack is brought and Netterville thanks him, taking the wine. Baker said that Netterville should have a room by himself with an aired bed.

Lord Netterville died later of his wounds. Colonel Talbot arrives upon the scene in a handbarrow. Talbot was a near relation of Tyrconnel and was usually called Wicked Will Talbot. Baker says that Talbot was lucky that the soldiers did not knock him on the head, and that he wished he had his cousin Tyrconnel in the room. The garrison would have been fully justified in showing no mercy to its prisoners, and at this point the Town Mayor enters to explain that he has just come from searching Ramsay's body. He found Hamilton's order in his pocket with the words written that there should be 'no quarter'.

Chapter 17

The Siege Intensifies

There was a lull after the battle of Windmill Hill, due according to Walker, to want of courage in the Catholic camp and a want of horses in the Protestant camp. The big mortars had not yet arrived, but the bombing still went on. The little cannons that were being used were not all that effective.

Small skirmishes took place outside the walls on most days. The garrison's morale was now very high, and they were now obsessed with the idea of dominating 'no-man's-land'. If any Catholics were seen to be approaching the walls, one or two of the garrison officers, with Captain Adam Noble of Lisnaskea, usually taking the lead, would sally forth and drive them away. Sometimes the other ranks sallied as well without waiting for their officers. If any soldiers on the walls saw their men get into difficulties, they would sally and these tactics helped to demoralize the Catholics.

The garrison intercepted a Jacobite post to Dublin at the end of May. The letters revealed that 3,000 of the besiegers had been killed or died of disease in the six weeks since their arrival at Londonderry and that they could get no rest due to the frequent Protestant sallies. The Catholics had dug trenches to shield themselves from the Protestant fire, but these measures were not enough. The only officers of the garrison to be killed in these skirmishes were Captain Cunningham and Lieutenant Douglas. Both of these officers were believed to have been murdered after surrendering on promise of receiving quarter.

Of the many outrages that took place, there was one that involved Lord Galmoy's dragoons. Galmoy was described by one contemporary as 'a monster whom no title could ennoble'. Treacherous behaviour according to Walker, was very common in the Catholic camp. This was admitted by a Catholic prisoner of war who was sufficiently troubled by his conscience as to confess that the Irish had taken an oath to abuse their Protestant prisoners. This only confirmed what the garrison suspected, and it made them more determined than ever to hold out against the Catholics. The Protestants were determined to hold out and they were convinced that the Catholics would not keep their promises.

The garrison was satisfied with what had been achieved in the first few weeks of the siege, but now they had troubles of their own. Colonel Parker had deserted to the Catholics, and now Colonel Whitney, another regimental commander, was in disgrace. His downfall had started with the arrival of a questionable

105

character called Captain Nicholas Darcy, who had been brought to Londonderry from Scotland by James Hamilton. He had been promptly arrested as a deserter from King William's service. Darcy managed to extort a promise from one of the Governors to leave Londonderry, complete with arms and one or more horses. It came to light that Darcy had brought the horses, together with a parcel of flour, from Colonel Whitney, and that the horses, had not been Whitney's to sell. Whitney was promptly court-martialled, and was found guilty of being no friend of the garrison. He was imprisoned for the remainder of the siege, and Captain Monro was promoted to take command of his regiment.

In May, a quarrel took place between Governor Henry Baker and Colonel John Mitchelburne, a brave hero of the siege. Walker however does not mention the incident, although it closely concerned the two men who were to be his colleagues in the Governorship. The cause of the quarrel remains a mystery. Ash notes in his diary that there were some sharp words between Baker and Mitchelburne, but does not say what they were about. Mackenzie after saying that Mitchelburne was suspected by Baker and the garrison, dismisses the incident as 'too tedious to relate'. The cause of the affair was probably due to the pressures that were building up behind the walls. However it seems that Mitchelburne was always loyal to the Protestant cause. Perhaps there was an argument of strategy or tactics, in which Mitchelburne had very definite views. There is no doubt that there were sharp words and that swords were drawn and that Mitchelburne was wounded by Baker, and that Mitchelburne was ordered under house arrest, but he was never tried by a Council of War. On Baker's deathbed, he was reduced to occupy a distinguished position. *Londerias* dismisses the whole affair:–

> They likewise Col'nel Mitchelburne confine
> And by good laws their government maintain.

The 'they' referred to was the new 'Council of Fourteen', set up about mid-May to assist and act as a check upon the Governors' powers; up till May they had enjoyed almost unlimited authority. This move seems to have resulted by dissatisfaction with Governor Walker. Mackenzie says that a hundred officers, including four regimental colonels, with Adam Murray amongst them, signed charges against Walker. This included allegations of selling or embezzling the stores, of abusing officers who went to the stores to obtain supplies, of attempting to betray the town and of attempting to betray it for money. Baker was diplomatic in his handling of the crisis, persuading the discontented to drop their charges against Walker and at the same time accepting the need of a governing Council. This Council was to consist of the regimental colonels automatically making Baker and Walker members. In addition to these, the Council was to consist of the Mayor Gervais Squire, and Alderman Cocken to represent the city and Archdeacon Jennings and Captain James Gladstone (or Gladstanes) to represent the surrounding countryside. Mogridge was appointed Secretary and Baker was elected President.

In future nothing was to be done unless seven members of the Council agreed. This was done to prevent any one man — even Baker — from surrendering the city to the Catholics. They might succeed where Lundy had failed. Throughout the siege, the garrison was to be distracted by rumours of treachery in high places, and as we have seen, even Walker's loyalty was sometimes suspected. These stories did not lack all foundation, for there were many in Londonderry who were defeatists and at worst Jacobites at heart. There were others — perhaps a majority — whose first priority was to survive, the unheroic ones. They ran to the bastions to do their bit of fighting with an apparent show of bravery.

There was 'Cowards' Bastion', so-called because it lay least out of danger. There was always a possibility that the cowards would gain the upper hand and jump at the chance of surrendering the town to James.

On 16th May, many of the citizens tried to parley with the enemy; this was an unauthorised meeting which the Governors broke up with gunfire from the walls. Nor was it thought safe to entrust the night watch to a single regiment. The guard therefore was made up of detachments from every battalion, so that each might keep a wary eye on the rest. Parker had deserted, Whitney was under close arrest and Mitchelburne was confined to his quarters. Also two captains had escaped from Londonderry, taking refuge with the Catholics.

Mitchelburne said that Hamilton was in daily correspondence with the people of Londonderry, and that his promises of clemency were being eagerly taken up, for between twenty and thirty people were leaving the town each day. Avaux claimed that this figure soon rose to between fifty and a hundred. The garrison's leaders did little to check this situation, probably acting on the knowledge that it was better to get rid of the faint-hearted and to save their supplies. They were not, at this point in time, worried about the knowledge that might get into the enemy's hands. James had come to the same conclusion and warned Hamilton that it was absolutely necessary that he should not let any more of the Protestants leave the city, for they would be glad to get rid of the excess mouths and thus prolong the siege of the city for the Catholics.

Avaux also saw it as the best plan not to let any more Protestants leave Londonderry, and that it was best to starve the garrison into surrender. However Hamilton did not listen to James's orders, and Protestants continued to make an exodus. James was convinced that Londonderry could be easily reduced, and he wrote to Hamilton that he would send as many men as possible to effect a surrender. Moreover he said that the Duke of Tyrconnel was preparing to go north to assist matters, but Tyrconnel never went. Rosen came instead.

To people living in Dublin, the siege did not seem to be going well at all. Wounded soldiers, carried in litters, started to arrive in the capital, after the repulse of Windmill Hill and the losses at Pennyburn. News of the Protestant victories at these places was received with great dismay. Londonderry began to be regarded as King James's slaughterhouse, with Avaux expressing the fear that James would have all his troops wiped out at the siege. Hamilton was winning no laurels, and this is made clear in Mitchelburne's play, in which the scene is the Catholic camp before Londonderry.

An EXPRESS came from Dublin for General Hamilton to read, and said that the king was dissatisfied with Hamilton's slow progress, and with the defeats which he had experienced. It said that Marshal Rosen was marching to besiege Enniskillen with 10,000 men and that he would advance to join Hamilton at Londonderry. His Majesty would be impatient until the town was reduced, for without the defeat of the Protestants, the Catholic cause was lost. The 800 men sent to the Highlands were now with Dundee, and that Edinburgh Castle was now safely in the hands of the Duke of Gordon. The letter was signed 'Melfort'. Hamilton digested the letter and exclaimed in anger that famine and plague had lit upon Londonderry, a 'perverse town, and that the besieged gloried in their ability to rebel.

May drew on without any further major engagements. The bombardment continued and provided occasional excitement, as when a red-hot ball came up Pump Street and broke the leg of one boy and wounded another before hitting the church wall.

About 20th May, the Catholics moved their main camp forward from St Johnston to Balloughry Hill, a point about two and a half miles south-west of the city. The siege was tightening and from now on, according to Walker, the Protestants would not send messages from the city. The supply of drinking water was threatened; the Foyle was tidal to beyond the town, and the only supply of water within Londonderry was so muddy and distasteful with the continual firing, with so many attempting to drink it.

The Protestants had taken to drawing water from Saint Columb's wells, just outside the walls. These wells were now under fire by the Catholics, and water could only be obtained at the expense of wood. One gentleman had a bottle broken at his mouth by the firing.

As yet there was little fear of a shortage of food, for by the end of May the horse mill at the free school began to grind malt; if the Protestants had been expecting famine, they would not have had any grain available for malting.

Good news came from Enniskillen, for early in May twelve companies of infantry and a few troops of horse had gone forward from the town to rout the Catholics at Belleek and relieve Ballyshannon. Patrick Sarsfield, commander of the Jacobite forces in those parts, was so obsessed with this threat to his rear, that he was never able to effectively bring his forces to relieve Londonderry. The Enniskillen men thought that they had been tricked by Sarsfield over an exchange of prisoners, but this is unlikely, for Sarsfield was a chivalrous man. The Enniskillen men however were fierce fighters, and it was after this incident that the Enniskillen men showed no mercy to the Catholics. Horror stories still piled in about Catholic atrocities to stiffen Protestant resistance.

At Belnahatty, Lord Galmoy's dragoons had again been playing football with men's heads in the streets, this time those of two Protestant gentlemen who had been taken in arms, hanged and then decapitated. There was the story of the unlucky peasants of Kilkerry, a little village near Omagh, who had set out one day to get back twenty or thirty cows, which had been stolen by two soldiers of the Irish garrison at Omagh. They recovered their cattle, but the two thieves made their way back to Omagh to complain to the garrison, which then set out to teach the villagers a lesson. A bog was nearby, and three of the villagers took refuge in it. The Catholic horse was unable to follow them there. The other five peasants surrendered on the promise of quarter, and they could not be blamed for recovering their own property.

The Catholic troopers were enraged at not being able to get at the peasants in the bog. At this they took their Protestant prisoners a short distance down the road and barbarously murdered them, cutting their faces so much that their friends could not recognize them when they came across them. This was the usual treatment meted out to Protestant prisoners, which was the principal reason why the Protestants of Londonderry and Enniskillen held out.

There was also the fate of one poor old crone of over seventy. She had been told that the Catholics were civil to visitors. She went along to their camp to try her luck, for she was told that they were well stocked with provisions. On her way, she was passed by a horseman carrying a sack of oatmeal, which burst and spilt its contents onto the road. The old lady gingerly grasped at the oatmeal, trying to separate it from the horse dung. Some superstitious fool thought she was a witch and put her to death.

Some time later, two Enniskillen Protestants, a clergyman called Andrew Hamilton and a Justice of the Peace, Anthony Dobbin, rode into the Catholic camp with a message from Richard Hamilton. They asked the meaning of this killing, and they were told that it was good sport and that an English or maybe a Scottish witch had been caught collecting their horses' dung and that she was intent upon destroying them — the Catholics — by her magic. Hamilton vainly tried to get some Irish officers to interfere, and Dobbin hurried in the direction of the firing squad and found the poor old lady lying on the ground. The Catholics were firing at her wildly and they had not yet killed her. One of the soldiers, before Dobbin could stop him, put the muzzle of his musket against her breast and shot her dead. The Protestants were incensed at Catholic cruelty of this kind. It was said that superstitious Catholics imagined that an old woman could destroy a contingent or turn the fate of a battle.

On 30th May, the great guns arrived outside Londonderry from Dublin to play their part in the siege. Until now little had been done by the Catholics to seriously effect a surrender by force of arms. It had been a long haul from Dublin, and the guns might have got to Derry sooner if they had been sent by sea, as James had first intended. This was dangerous since there were English vessels about. James was still pressing for the siege to go ahead, and he armed his troops with all speed possible and sent to Londonderry those that were best armed. Colonel Buchan was ordered to bring his troops from County Down up to Londonderry.

Steps were now taken so that the English could not relieve Londonderry by sea. Some said that the best way to do this was to sink ships in the navigable channel of the River Foyle. It was decided that this was not the best course of action, since it would ruin the maritime trade of the town which would soon be in Jacobite hands. The French artillery expert, the Marquis de Pointis was ordered to block the channel of the river with a floating boom. By 4th June, after one false start, he had completed the task. There was a narrow point in the river at Brookhall, and here the boom was sited.

Walker says that the Catholics tried to place a boom of timber, joined by iron chains and fortified by a cable twelve inches thick twisted round it. The boom was first of all made out of oak, but that could not float and was soon broken by the water. Then they made one of fir beams, which was fastened at one end through the arch of a bridge, and at the other end by a piece of timber forced into the ground and fortified by a piece of stonework. News about the beam reached the garrison by prisoners of war, and Walker said that the news of the beam upset and scared the citizens of the city.

Pointis said that he was not given sufficient materials to complete the task, and that he commanded beams of timber a foot square from nearby houses. These were joined together by iron cramps which allowed the boom to float up and down with the force of the tides. From the shore the boom was covered by semicircular entrenchments dug one above another in the form of an amphitheatre on the steep left bank. From these trenches the Catholics were able to fire their way across the boom.

Pointis was confident that no enemy ships could hack their way across the boom with hatchets. He was pleased with his work, and he declared that the only thing that would enhance his achievement was that the English would be so foolish as to try to break the boom. The English could only do this with the help of a following wind, and if they get stuck on it, they could not turn back, and they would be caught by the Catholic pistol fire from the shore. Pointis sat back to await the English moves, having completed the boom just in time.

Four days before the boom was completed, the English fleet had sailed down the Mersey. The Londonderry garrison, confident that a relief expedition was on the way, were in the meanwhile able to achieve another victory at Windmill Hill. Here on 4th June, the Catholics tried to reverse the result of a previous engagement. This had made the Protestants in possession of the Windmill entrenchments. Richard Hamilton was determined to humiliate the Protestants and to curb their spirit of rebellion. A considerable force was assembled in front of the Windmill line, twelve battalions of infantry and fifteen or sixteen squadrons of horse. It was planned that the cavalry would attack from the right, advancing in three successive moves down the Foyle. By then it was low tide. The main body of infantry was to advance on the cavalry's left and attack the Windmill entrenchments. A second column of foot would attack the lines at the Bogside, between the Windmill and the city.

The Protestants learnt what was afoot and marched out of the city in strength to man the trenches. All were set for what was to prove the most important battle of the siege. *Hussa* was the Catholic battle cry, as the horse and foot began to advance. This shout was seconded from all parts of their camp with dreadful shrieks and shouting. On the right part of the Jacobite cavalry, armed cap-a-pie — and led by Lord Mountgarret's second son — they had bound themselves by an oath to take the Protestant entrenchments. They came rushing along the strand to attack the garrison's men, and Ash admitted that they did this with great courage.

The garrison had been asked to hold their fire until the last moment; they confronted the Catholics with a volley of fire and were surprised by what little damage this did. Captain Crooke, realizing that the bullets were not penetrating the troopers' cuirasses, ordered his men to aim at the horses, which fell in struggling heaps. The Catholics then retreated in confusion. Those Catholics which did manage to make the Protestant defences, found themselves confronted by a dry bank seven foot high at the Waterside. Most of them found that this was too high for the cavalry.

Butler himself, well-mounted, led the way; he spurred his horse and flew over the bank, but he was at once taken prisoner. Colonel Purcell, who followed Butler, had his horse killed and only saved himself by a quick jump backwards. Another gallant old soldier Edward Butler, who reached the bank, was killed. Of the thirty Catholics that made the spot, only three escaped, and the rest were either killed or made prisoner by being hauled over the bank by the hair of their heads.

The Catholic infantry had fared no better in the centre. They had begun their advance with a stately line of colonels heading the way, pike in hand. The front rank had been ordered to march with bundles of brushwood or faggots held in front of them as a protection against the enemy fire. The Protestants placed themselves within their lines in three ranks, so that one rank could march up and relieve the other, and discharge their pistols upon the Catholics. The Catholics thought that the Protestants would make a single volley and fall in upon them. Even regular troops needed constant exercise to combat this sort of successive firing and there must have been plenty of good instructors in Londonderry.

Despite these tactics, the Catholics managed to make their way to the Protestant entrenchments, only to find them too high to be stormed. This could only be done with scaling ladders, of which they had none. The Catholics found the Protestant musket fire too strong and the faggot men were unable to stand before the garrison's shot. The Catholics were forced to run. The grenadiers on the left came nearest to success, and they had advanced over the bogland near the Double Bastion. They drove back the garrison's outpost from the trenches, which they climbed only to find one defender confronting them. This was a small boy who pelted them with stones.

Governor Baker directed the defence with considerable skill, and he quickly restored the situation by calling up reserves to counterattack. But now the Catholics found themselves confronting a new enemy in the women of Londonderry. Mackenzie says that the women also did 'good service', for they

111

carried ammunition, match, bread, and drink to their men. They threw stones at the Catholics; these were taken up from the streets to deaden the fall of shells. In *Ireland Preserved* there is a generous tribute made to the Protestants by Richard Hamilton, who said that they were men of undaunted resolution, and were much bolder than his Catholic forces. They had aimed their guns with great effect. In *Ireland Preserved* three Amazons enter the scene — 'Deborah Betitia, leading a Captain of the Irish Guard, a prisine; also Felicia and Gertrude with one of the enemy's colour she took'. They were almost breathless, and said that if they each had a pair of breeches, they would have been in pursuit. The references to breeches and petticoats no doubt drew laughter from the audience.

The battle was decided within a few hours, and the Catholics were retreating in defeat. Murderous fire had destroyed the enemy's horses, the cavalry wheeling back also in defeat. The Protestants leapt forward from their redoubts to chase the Catholics with pike and musket, whilst the 'shavers' did terrible damage with their scythes. Many of the Catholic troops were killed and others driven into the Foyle to drown due to the weight of their armour. The 'faggot men' had found their brushwood an inadequate protection against the Protestant fire, and they were in full retreat. They ran away slowly, for they were carrying dead men on their backs to shield their bodies from enemy bullets. Walker said that the corpses had performed a more useful function dead than they had alive.

The Catholic grenadiers were being chased over the bogs by Deborah Betitia, Felicia, Gertrude and other screaming women, who pounded them with stones. The Protestants had only six private soldiers killed and one official, Captain Maxwell; his arm was blown off by a cannon shot from across the river. According to Walker, the Catholics lost 400 men, and Ash reported that they had about 150 wounded — information gained from prisoners. But *Londerias* says that:–

Then reinforced, we chase them o'er the plain,
Where full two thousand of their men were slain.

However it is thought that the Catholic casualties had not been nearly so heavy. It was one of those battles in which the casualties of the side that turned and ran were greater than those of the victors. There was the usual high proportion of officers amongst the casualties — nine killed, ranging from a lieutenant colonel to ensign, and six or seven taken prisoner. Some put the figure much higher, for Pointis reported that there were some forty officers killed or wounded in the Catholic camp.

There was a post mortem on the Catholic side into this serious defeat. Pointis thought that the main reason for the defeat was that the battle plan was altered at the last moment. Hamilton had let his judgement be crowded by other officers, who had assured him that they could win without losing twenty men. It was said that the battle was undertaken contrary to every kind of rule and without paying heed to what Hamilton had ordered. The casualties were not the worst part of the affair, but that there was a general despondency amongst the troops. More than 300 soldiers had deserted, particularly from Nugent's regiment. The Catholics came to the conclusion that the only way of defeating the Protestants was for them to await on hunger. Attacking the Protestants was no longer thought of as a wise policy. Blame was put on the poor quality of the Catholic soldiers. Avaux had thought that the Windmill was an easy post to capture. He reported to Hames that the troops had behaved badly. Plunket said that the Protestants had more fight in them, and more skill, than all the officers of the Catholic army. King James was becoming a workman that was more and more ready to blame his tools, and blamed the defeat of the Catholic infantry on not putting their whole heart into the matter.

The garrison attributed their victory to God, who was watching over Protestant efforts. Captain Ash, who had shown great bravery in the Windmill battle commented in his diary:– 'Blessed be God! We had a notable victory over them, to their great discouragement, for they have not attempted a place since'.

The garrison returned to the city in great spirits, and they were further encouraged by the news that the relieving force was on its way to the Foyle. On 31st May, four days before the battle at the Windmill, a fleet of thirty ships had sailed from Liverpool, carrying 5,000 troops and a great stock of food. It was under the command of Major General Percy Kirke.

Chapter 18

Kirke's Dilemma

General Kirke was a soldier of twenty-three years' experience, and was forty-three years of age. He had received his commission from James when he was Duke of York. He had begun his military career as an ensign in the yellow-coated Maritime Regiment, the forerunner of the Royal Marines. However he did not achieve any great distinction until 1681, when he commanded the 2nd Tangier Regiment in the city of Tangier. A year later he became Governor of the place for the last three years of its existence as a British colony. He took over command of the Governor's Regiment, whose badge was the Pascal Lamb. This regiment had a reputation for great ferocity and it was nicknamed 'Kirke's Lambs'. He brought his men back to England in time to fight for James at Sedgemoor, when he became notorious for his treatment of Monmouth's rebels after the battle. He favoured the sign of an inn for a gibbet, and it was from the sign of the White Hart in Taunton, where he was billeted, that he managed to string up a number of soldiers in sight of the inn's windows. When the dying men's legs twisted in their last moments, Kirke ordered drums to start beating. There was no punishment from James for such cruelty, and the king only chided him, for James himself had given the order for the rebels to be put to death. The Tangier soldiers found Kirke's behaviour all very good sport. Kirke later gained credit for putting more than a hundred prisoners to death in the week following Sedgemoor. He did not miss the opportunity to feather his own nest and when he was recalled from the West Country, it was not because of his cruelty but because of his leniency towards rich criminals.

In the eyes of contemporaries, Kirke had an ugly reputation, and Whig historians, amongst them Macaulay, have not been kind to him. Burnet said that he had commanded in Tangier so long that he had become a barbarian. Samuel Pepys found Kirke quite intolerable, when he visited Tangier in 1683 to wind up the affairs of the colony. He said that Kirke was a drunken lout who commanded a drunken regiment. Pepys was reviled by Kirke and his men. There were endless dirty stories told at the Governor's table, which passed from the 'distasteful to the unendurable'. Pepys withdrew from Kirke's Mess and dined alone. To Pepys the Governor's administration appeared to be both cruel and corrupt. There were stories of soldiers being beaten to death and Jewish refugees returned to the tortures of the Spanish Inquisition. There were stories of rape and robberies and bullying of the citizens and their wives. It must be said that Kirke more than any other man had improved Tangier's defences.

After the battle of Sedgemoor, Kirke continued to serve James as an officer of the regular army. He noticed with annoyance that all promotions were going to Catholics. Kirke decided that if he could not beat them, he would join them. However he did not change his religion and said that he had promised the Emperor of Morocco, that if he ever renounced the Protestant faith, it would be to become a Mussalman.

Kirke marched westwards with the royal army when William landed at Torbay; he loudly proclaimed that he would shed the last drop of his blood for King James. However he quickly changed sides, and William promoted him to the rank of Major General within three days.

Kirke set about the relief of Londonderry half-heartedly. His orders from Whitehall had been issued on 28th April and his troops started to assemble at the port of Liverpool, whilst the brewers and bakers there and at Chester were set to work at preparing provisions. King William was annoyed that Kirke was hanging around Merseyside, and he had to be prodded into activity by a sharp note for Lord Shrewsbury.

Kirke now set into action, and sailed down the Mersey only to be driven back by a contrary wind. It was not until 31st May, that his fleet finally got underway. There was however more bad weather and he was forced to seek shelter in the Isle of Man, where a number of men, having fled from Ulster, went on board to offer their services. Bad weather also meant that he had put in at Rathlin Island, off the North Coast. Here he requisitioned 100 head of cattle. On board were four regiments of infantry, his own Lambs, Sir John Hammer's men, and those of Colonels Cunningham and Richards. George Rooke commanded the horse contingent. Among his subordinates was Captain Leake, who was in command of the frigate *Dartmouth*.

Kirke had sent a reconnaissance force ahead of his main force. The ships which were chosen were all shallow draught that could make their way up the Foyle. There was the frigate *Greyhound*, the ketch *Fisher* and the merchant ketch *Edward and James*. On board of these ships were a lieutenant, an ensign and forty soldiers, including gunners and miners; the army's senior representative was Captain Jacob Richards. Richards was ordered to go no more than a cannon's shot off the fort of Culmore, his main task being to gather intelligence about the state of affairs in Londonderry, and whether the river channel had been blocked. He was told that under no circumstances was he to venture up the Foyle if the channel had been blocked.

The garrison kept watch from the walls and the Cathedral tower. On 7th June they saw the masts of the *Greyhound* and the other ships. They wanted to send a welcoming party down the Foyle, but the rowlocks had been placed so close together that they could not row. Meanwhile some gentlemen had told Richards that the Catholics had indeed placed a boom across the Foyle at

Brookhall. They were Mr Newton, Mr Gage and Mr Cunningham, who had been living under the enemy's protection in pleasant houses along the lough's shore.

It was at this time that Richards noticed that the Catholics were trying to sink a boat loaded with stone in the Foyle, in order to block it. They had been pulling down a house near Culmore and were carrying away stones and rubbish. Captain Guillan commanded the *Greyhound*, and Richards now ordered that she should move more closer in to Culmore Fort, where she dropped anchor. The *Greyhound* proceeded to engage the Catholics on the shore with her guns. It is difficult to see what Richards hoped to gain by this move. The Catholics bombarded the frigate from both shores with 24-pounders, 8-pounders and 3-pounders, and the *Greyhound* was the worse for it, for the ship ran aground and the tide fell. She was stranded on the southern shore, and she was heeled over so that her guns could not aim at the enemy. It was only the brisk musketry fire that deterred the Catholics from boarding her.

The engagement went on for about seven hours, and by then the frigate had about four or five feet of water in her hold. She had been hit seventeen times below the water line, and severe damage had been done to the masts and rigging. It was thought that the best plan was to abandon ship. The lifeboats had only rowed about a quarter of a mile from the frigate when the wind suddenly changed and she refloated. The crew went back on board, and the ship eventually made its way back to Scotland for refitting and repair.

The Catholics took great pleasure in letting the Protestants know of the disaster of the *Greyhound*, the first of their deliverers. The Catholics said that the Protestants should send carpenters down river to repair her. The *Greyhound* should have been battered to bits but for the fact that the Catholic gunners were a bad aim. Captain Richards lost all his possessions to the value of £300, and what had not been destroyed by the enemy, had been looted by his own men.

Richards transferred to the *Portland* to await the arrival of Major General Kirke and the main body. The besieged had been overjoyed to see the arrival of the *Greyhound* and her two little sister ships, but they were overwhelmed when they saw on the 11th June the arrival of Kirke's fleet in the Foyle. It was ten times as numerous and included Rook's powerful contingent of naval warships. For a short while the garrison were under the impression that all their troubles were over and they rang the cathedral bells in triumph; they also fired off three cannon shots to which the fleet made a reply. It was said later that the arrival of Kirke's fleet was heralded by a sign in the daytime sky, a sort of Star of Bethlehem, and which was interpreted by Londonderry's men as a sign of imminent relief.

The Catholics were alarmed at the arrival of Kirke's fleet, and their first thought was to raise the siege in the next twenty-four hours. This the garrison learnt from a deserter named Dobin or Dolan. The Catholics could be seen from the walls beginning to strike their tents, while many of their troops threw away their red tunics and decamped. The relieving expedition was undecided what to do, and this bewildered the Catholics and alarmed the Protestants. Kirke proceeded to do nothing; his ships were in the lough below Culmore, but they might as well have been sitting at Bristol or Liverpool as far as help to the Protestants was concerned.

The Catholics, seeing that the fleet was not coming up the river, took heart and reoccupied their former positions on the river bank. Walker said that the Catholics proceeded to watch the garrison more carefully:– 'They now began to watch as narrowly. They raise battalions opposite to the ships and line both sides of the river with great numbers of firelocks'. Guns were also posted at Charlesfort, a place of some strength upon the narrow part of the river, from which they could give additional covering fire to the boom from the southern shore.

Kirke had arrived in the Foyle with no definite plans of how he should relieve Londonderry. It is not known if he had taken any steps to inform himself of conditions in the region. He could have presumably consulted Cunningham and Richards, even though they were disgraced, but there is no indication that he did so. Although he had with him officers of the two regiments of the April fiasco, their brief visit to Londonderry would not have put them in a position to give him much useful information. There were now two options open to Kirke, and it seems that he decided to make battle plans when he was on the spot. The obvious, and perhaps the best plan, of getting relief to Londonderry was to send his shallow-draught ships up the Foyle to smash their way through Pointis's boom and reach the Ship Quay. Marshal Rosen, for the Catholic side, thought that he might easily have done this. Kirke was obsessed with the idea that his ships might be exposed to some danger as they passed through the Culmore Narrows, where the channel was less than one hundred yards wide and where Catholic gunners could hardly miss. If the ships survived the cannon fire at Culmore, they would still have to face the boom at Brookhall. Kirke was also convinced that the Catholics had sunk boats full of stones and rubbish in the Foyle, but this seems unlikely, although one source states that the Catholics did sink boats and placed spikes in the riverbed.

The threat of the boom was real enough, and Jacob Richards who was sent to take a look at it, reported back that it bobbed up and down in the water like some sort of prehistoric sea monster. To send his ships up the river seemed to Kirke a great risk, and eventually he got round to the alternative, which was to take his fleet out of Lough Foyle and sail round the Inishowen Peninsula into Lough Swilly, and make a headquarters at Inch Island. Inch lay at the head of the lough and was convenient both to Londonderry and Enniskillen. Sailing into Lough Swilly might expose his ships to far less risk. On the other hand he would be as far from Derry at Inch Island as he was at Culmore. He would have to take food to Londonderry and this meant assembling wagons and horses. To get there he would have to fight his way through the Catholic army. To achieve this he had only three regiments, his own Lambs, Steuart's and Hanmer's.

Dalrymple states that Kirke's three regiments totalled 5,000 men, but another writer, Storey, gives the strength of the Lambs at 666, of Hanmer's 593 and of Steuart's 660. Numbers would be more formidable if an attack by Kirke could be synchronized by an attack from the garrison. Communications were not at their best and a synchronised attack would have been difficult. There would be delay if he approached by Lough Swilly, and already the House of Commons in London was beginning to ask questions why there was such delay. One member cried that this was not the time to be counting cost, and that if these brave fellows in Londonderry were not relieved, then all the world would cry shame upon England. There was no excuse for not breaking the boom; England's kith and kin were to perish only a few hours' sailing from her shores.

Kirke was not sure how badly the city was off for food and what was the state of her defences. Garrison and fleet could see each other quite clearly for Captain Richards was not the only one that possessed a prospect glass. They however had not learnt how to communicate with each other. The navies in Europe had worked out systems of signalling with flags and lights. Codes had been devised which depended upon the number and position of flags or lights, or the number of shots fired. There was no one in Londonderry who was familiar with these skills. The fleet misinterpreted the garrison's amateurish efforts at signalling. When no signals were made, Kirke assumed that no news was good news. When the garrison waved a banner four times from the steeple to indicate they were in bad straits, Kirke thought they were boastfully waving enemy standards.

Kirke weighed up the risks of sending his ships up the Foyle, and he found that he was in a bit of a dilemma. Kirke did not like the idea of facing the Catholic guns, which were probably as powerful as his own. Kirke had to depend upon wind and tide. He was unaware of the few guns that the Catholics had and how indifferent were the gunners who manned the cannon. He had a false idea of the strength of the boom. Avaux was well aware of its weaknesses; he reported to Louis that it had been weakly constructed, and that it was often broken by force of wind and tide.

On the evening of 16th June, Kirke called together the pilots of the fleet and asked whether any of them would be willing to take a ship across the bow at the head of the lough. Kirke therefore did not immediately discard the thought of attempting the river passage. The pilots could not guarantee success, yet promised to do their best. The Major General thought about this advice for three days and he convened a full Council of War on board the *Swallow*. All the captains of the fleet, and all the colonels and lieutenant colonels of the army, were gathered together to discuss matters.

There was no news from Londonderry and this was used as an excuse for making the hazardous journey to the city and to break the boom. After much debate, after which the several obstacles against proceeding to Derry were discussed at some length, a unanimous resolution was forwarded to Schomberg, King William's commander in chief designate; this was based upon the assumption that boats had been sunk in the channel and that the garrison's condition was as yet by no means desperate. The fleet first of all was aware that a boom and a chain had been placed across the river about Brookhall and were also aware that boats had been sunk in the channel. Also, the town of Londonderry had not sent any word to Kirke about their condition, which in the opinion of the Council of War was reason to believe that they were not threatened by the Catholics, nor did they want provisions. They thought it the best place to remain in Lough Swilly until further reinforcements arrived from England and Scotland. Kirke thought that it was only best, in the short term, to make a move if the garrison needed it.

The besieged were bewildered and exasperated by Kirke's inactivity. Their food supplies had only been briefly augmented by the flesh of horses killed at the second battle of Windmill Hill. These they salted down, but now provisions were running low. The townsfolk were weak with hunger and disease, and they were dying like flies. Ash says that throughout the siege there was an average of thirty deaths a day. One day alone, as many as fifteen officers died.

The death rate in the Catholic camp was not as great in proportion to numbers. The season was unusually wet and cold, and a dry bed for the sick and wounded was a luxury enjoyed only by the few. Walker said that the besieged took longing looks towards the ships as their provisions ran low. A beacon was lit on the steeple as a sign of the town's distress, and *Londerias* said that:–

Yet all in vain, Kirke would not venture up;
Some say of usquebaugh he had got a cup.

The futile efforts to communicate went on and they made several signs from the steeple, but neither could make out each other's signals.

The oars on the rowing boat had now been altered, and two attempts were made to row it to the fleet, each attempt at which was beaten back by heavy fire from the Catholics. Instead it was decided to row the boat up to Donnalong Wood, and there land two small boys who were to bring word of the city's plight to Enniskillen. It is not known why children were thought suitable for the mission. A story was put about that the object of the mission was to raid some fish houses on an island in the river. Time had been allowed for this tale to reach the Catholics through some of the many deserters who were still leaving the city daily.

The boat set off after dusk, crewed by the intrepid Adam Murray and four other officers, with twenty other ranks. The Catholics were expecting them and the Protestants came under fire from their muskets and a great gun from Evan's Wood. The Protestants reached Donnalong, but the two small boys were too frightened to go ashore. Dawn was breaking and it was not realized that two of the men could go instead. The boat turned back to make the four-mile haul back to Londonderry, and she was intercepted by two boats full of Catholic muskets. There was an engagement in mid-stream, with both sides firing away without hurt to anyone. One of the Catholic boats closed in with the intention of boarding the Protestant craft, but Murray and his men knocked some of them on the head. They killed a lieutenant and several soldiers and took the remaining thirteen Catholics prisoner. The second Catholic boat at once pulled for the shore, and the Derry men, under fire from the shore, returned safely to the city, their only casualty being Adam Murray himself, who sustained a head wound.

Meanwhile Kirke had decided to establish communications by sending spies through the enemy lines into the city, a dangerous mission for which there were few volunteers. At length two men were found and sent forth. One of them returned to the ships a few days later only to report that he had got no further than the Catholic camp, where he had been turned back by the sentries, having been lucky enough not to have been arrested. Due to darkness, he had been separated from his friend. On the way back he had learnt that a spy had been captured and executed by the Catholics, and this he assumed had been his companion. After this discouraging start, it was difficult to find any more volunteers, and eventually a Scot named James Cromie threatened to make the attempt with a friend called James Roch. Cromie was a non-swimmer, but he knew the countryside and had come along to show the way to Roch, who was a very strong swimmer indeed, as events were to prove.

Mitchelburne says that Roch was Irish — and certainly Roch was a well-known Irish name — and he expresses surprise that none but a Catholic should be chosen for the dangerous mission. He hints that Roch's main concern was to assist the enemy. Roch was now to undergo a series of adventures which would try the stamina of a James Bond. The tale comes from his own account, later given to the House of Commons, when he was trying to obtain the reward promised to him by Kirke. It is certain that the tale does not err on the side of understatement.

Roch and Cromie were put ashore at ten o'clock one night at a place which Roch calls Faughan, and is presumably the place where the River Faughan runs into the Foyle from the southern shore, some five miles below Londonderry. Roch and Cromie trudged upstream through the night, and managed to pass the Catholic lines without being detected. Some time after midnight they arrived at a deserted fish house three miles above Londonderry. They were still on the wrong side of the river, so Roch stripped and slid into the icy waters of the Foyle to set out on the three miles' swim down to the town.

Roch came ashore at Londonderry at four o'clock in the morning, quite exhausted, feeling the cold. He was revived with strong liquor, but found that the citizens were intent upon hanging him as a spy. He persuaded them not to kill him until he made a prearranged signal from the cathedral steeple to the fleet. Richards says that this signal was the discharge of four guns from the tower at twelve o'clock noon. Roch was able to tell the garrison how the city would react to the signal, and when they did so he was accepted as one of the Protestants. He proceeded to tell the garrison of the arrangements made for their relief. According to Graham he brought a letter from Kirke saying that Kirke was bringing relief beyond their wildest dreams. Kirke exhorted them to save as much food as possible, an exhortion more terrible to the citizens than all the threats of the Catholics. Roch was asked by the citizens to return to the fleet and tell Kirke that they had only four days' provisions left. This Roch, despite his long swim to the city, agreed to do. He swam the whole way back to the fish house, reaching it at midnight, twenty-four hours after he had first left it and at once found himself surrounded by the Catholics, who had picked up Cromie earlier. They chased Roch stark-naked three miles through a wood until in desperation the poor man leapt into the Foyle from a thirty foot bluff. At the same time he had his jaw and collarbone broken from a halberd. The Catholic dragoons pursued him into the river, and crying out that he would be given quarter and a reward of £10,000 if he surrendered. Roch swam bravely on, and although a great number of shots were fired at him, he managed to reach Londonderry at four o'clock in the morning, with wounds to his chest, hand and shoulder. He lay unconscious for an hour, and he fully earned the reward of a captain's commission in William's army and a gift of lands on the Everard estates in County Waterford.

Cromie, too, had had his ups and downs and misadventures. He had seen Roch launched on his swim to Londonderry, and he had remained hidden for a day or two amongst the bushes on the bank. He waited hopefully for a boat which Roch had promised to send him. He was captured by the Catholics who brought him to Stronge's Orchard, where the Chevalier de Vaudry was ordered to give him a thorough interrogation.

James heard that Cromie was a man of good sense and that he spoke French perfectly, and that he had an income of 500 guineas a year. Under de Vaudry's threats he agreed to betray Kirke, and send the garrison a different message than that which the General had intended. With Cromie on their side, the Catholics hung out a white flag, inviting the Protestants to parlee. They said that the Protestants were mistaken about Kirke and the relief expedition from England. Lieutenant Colonels Blair and Fortescue went across the river to Stronge's Orchard to parlee with Lord Louth and Colonel O'Neill and to hear what Cromie had to say. When Blair asked him why his story was different from Roch's, he replied that he was a prisoner in the enemy's hands while Roch was in Londonderry. However the two colonels soon discovered that Cromie was cheating.

Roch and Cromie were to have returned to the spot where they had originally been put ashore. On the night of 26th June, the fleet, aware of what was happening to the two men, sent a boat to pick them up at Faughan. The Catholics, probably alerted by Cromie, were waiting at the spot and shouted through the darkness to the boat's crew to come in to land. They were unable to give a password or name the ship to which the two spies should return. The boat pulled away to get safely back to the fleet, where it was assumed that the two men had been captured. Signalling attempts still continued between the cathedral steeple and fleet.

At about this time, a man called McGimsey went to Adam Murray with an offer to swim down the Foyle with a message to the fleet. On 26th June, at ten o'clock at night, McGimsey started to swim from Ship Quay, carrying three letters to Kirke, which were tied around his neck in a bladder. The bladder was weighed down with musket balls, so that if he were captured, he could cut the string, and the bladder would sink. But McGimsey was never seen alive again, and a day or two later the Catholics displayed his body from a gallows, after calling out across the river. McGimsey was not hanged, but had been drowned, and hanging might well have been his fate if he had been taken alive. He was probably killed by being dashed against the boom by the force of the water. He had not had time to cut the string around his neck, so that the bladder, together with the letters, fell into Catholic hands.

Rosen, who had just returned to Londonderry, wrote to James that they had managed to fish a man out of the Foyle with bladders about his arms. He said that he found the bladder about the neck of the drowned man and that the letter had come into his possession. Rosen sent the letters to James, so that the king could see what state the town was in. The besiegers took great encouragement upon reading the letters. One of the letters, signed by Baker, Walker and Mitchelburne said that the Protestants were running out of provisions and the town would have to be surrendered within six or seven days. They learnt from the letters that they — the Protestants — understood that the boom was broken, so that Kirke could make the voyage up the Foyle with ease. However neither of these statements were correct. The boom was not broken, and the citizens of Londonderry were able to hold out for a further six weeks under conditions of ever-increasing starvation.

Chapter 19

Londonderry Stands Firm

The sight of the English ships lying in the Foyle was tantalizing, and this heightened the tension in Londonderry, and caused 'the rabble' to turn nasty. However the immediate cause of the trouble was a man called Wicked Will Talbot, who was lying a prisoner in Derry. He had been present at the first Windmill battle over a month earlier. His wounds were not improving, despite the fact that the garrison had done their best for him. He was sick and nearing death. His wife came up from the South to be with him, and she sent a trumpeter to the walls to offer a ransom of £500 for his release. The Council of Fourteen met to consider her offer. Baker had been too ill to leave his room, and a heated debate took place in the Council. Everyone except Baker agreed upon reaching terms, and they said that Madam Talbot would be better sending bullocks rather than cash as a ransom. But the Council would have been quite willing to see Wicked Will free if only the garrison were allowed to send a message down the river to Kirke, but this, as it transpired, was not possible. But the mob shouted that they would only accept prisoners for him and not money, for money was of little practical value within the walls.

Baker realized the strength of popular feeling, for he overrode the Council's decision. Wicked Will solved the problem for everyone by dying, with his wife by his bedside. Walker said that the city had now lost its bargaining position, and that they took as many measures as possible to keep Wicked Will alive. Will was allowed ample food and drink, favours agreed upon with the enemy, and this at a time when the garrison was short of provisions itself. Wicked Will was buried in Londonderry two days later. Some members of the Council wanted to keep Will's wife as a hostage, but chivalry prevailed and Will was escorted back to the Catholic camp.

Meanwhile the mob in Londonderry had been on the rampage. They sacked Walker's quarters and uncovered his private stock of beer and 'mum'. Mackenzie says that Walker brought this trouble on himself, when Baker vetoed the decision to release Wicked Will, Walker had been for releasing Will and ordered that a bier which would take him away be brought to his quarters. The mob was enraged by this and took the bier and burnt it in the main guard. Walker ignores this incident in his journal. He fled for safety to Baker's quarters and was hotly pursued by the mob. Some threatened to shoot him whilst others threatened to send him to jail.

Baker, though very ill, went out and pacified the mob. He said that there should be no ransom taken for the prisoners, and entreated them for his sake to overlook what Walker had done. He said that they should allow the prisoners to go to their lodgings again, and the mob consented that this should be so. Mackenzie said that he was not sure how the mob regarded the action of Walker.

The discovery of Walker's private stock of beer and 'mum' gave rise to the accusation amongst later Presbyterian writers that he was more fond of the bottle than his duties. There is very little evidence of a contemporary kind to support these charges. Mackenzie was his archenemy, and in one of his vague innuendoes, talks about vices attributed to Walker of a vague kind. One of these vices was said to be drunkenness according to Professor Killen, who published an edited version of Mackenzie's account in 1861. He said that Walker's morals caused great uneasiness during the siege. Witheroe slyly refers to Walker's 'little infirmity'. Thomas Hamilton, in *History of the Presbyterian Church,* published in 1887, says that Walker was fond of the glass. Another later source says that Walker's personal vices were, in all probability, drunkenness. Others say that Walker was fond of the bottle, and that otherwise he was a great man of peace.

'Mum' is described in the dictionary as a kind of beer originally brewed in Brunswick; the principal constituents of which were wheat-milk, oat-malt, ground beans, with tops of fir and birch, cardamum, Benetius, Rosaceous, Burnet, betony, marjoram, avens, pennyroyal, cardacum and bay berries. It was one of the most useful liquors under the sun, and was used to combat distempers, where there was a deprivation of blood in the bowels. It was a very heartening and strengthening drink. But it was troublesome to brew, with all those herbs, and it sounds more like a drunkard's delight than a health-giving beverage.

Internal quarrels in Londonderry came to a temporary standstill when news arrived that the formidable Rosen was back in the Catholic camp, now with the title of 'Marshal General of all His Majesties Forces'. He reached the city on 17th June, and expressed great hatred of the Protestants. He 'swore by the Belly of God he would demolish our favour and bury us in its Ashes, putting all to the Sword without consideration of age or sex, and would study the most exquisite Torments to lengthen the pain and misery of all he found obstinate or active in opposing his Commands and Pleasures'.

Rosen's threats had very little affect over the Protestants. In return Walker pronounced that any man talking about surrender of the city would be put to death. On his journey back to Londonderry, Rosen had been sending James a constant stream of grumbles and grievances, complaining of bad roads, of a shortage of weapons and of the number of desertions. Also he complained that Hamilton's men were too few in number and that they were poorly armed and worn out. Rosen reminded James that some time ago he had warned the king against laying siege to Londonderry with such a strength of men. He urged James to send reinforcements at his earliest opportunity. Rosen complained about his badly disciplined troops, the shortage of tents, forage, ammunition and other necessaries. When the letters, that had come into their possession by way of the dead McGimsey, revealed that the garrison had only six or seven days' food supply left, he was able to boast to James that "I told you so". He said that James would have been master of the town long ago if he had taken his advice. Rosen said that if the policy of not letting refugees out of Londonderry had been pursued, the town would have been reduced to surrender long ago.

Hamilton's more lenient policy had had its advantages for, as Graham said, desertions from the city now became frequent that the Catholics received constant information of what was going on. Desertions proved great trouble for the Governors.

Rosen's policies were tight, and he was now to pursue the tactics of assembling large numbers of Protestants under the walls of Derry, leaving them without food, so that the garrison would have to admit them to the city. Before this occurred the farcical interlude of Donough Macarthy, Lord Clancarty. Avaux described him as a little madcap, and he was a nephew of Macarthy, Lord Mountcashel. He arrived in Londonderry with his regiment at the end of June; there was an ancient family prophecy that a Clancarty should one day knock at the gates of Derry. This he decided to put to the test on the night of his arrival, given courage with the help of strong drink. Filled with Dutch courage, and one June evening, Clancarty came marching over the bog at Butcher's Gate. So vigorous was the attack, that he drove the defenders from their posts, and he managed to get some miners into a cellar under the half-bastion. At this the garrison reacted quickly. Adam Noble, with some companions, went out of Bishop's Gate, and crept along the walls until they ran across a covering party which Clancarty had posted to protect his miners. They held their fire until they were at close range, and then opened up with their guns. The defenders on the walls joined in the shouting with such intensity that Ash noted in his diary that he never heard so many shots fired at the same time. Clancarty left his miners to their fate and retreated back to the Catholic camp, leaving many of his best men dead behind him, a hundred of them, according to Walker, and about a third of this according to estimates made by Ash and Mackenzie.

The Protestants cheered at the Catholic retreat, pointing out that a Clancarty would only knock at the gates of Londonderry, and not that he would succeed in entering the city. The Catholics however had no monopoly on superstition, for the garrison's hopes of relief were being sustained by the firm belief that at midnight every night an angel was seen over the city, mounted on a snow-white horse and brandishing a sword of bright colour.

Governor Baker died a day or two after the repulse of Clancarty's raid. He had been out on the walls during the various conflicts and he had caught a succession of heavy colds which by the middle of June had turned into a violent fever, perhaps pneumonia, which forced him into his bed in the Bishop's Palace. He seemed to be getting better after a fortnight's rest, but at this point he heard that the Catholics were going to make a vigorous attack, probably Clancarty's. He insisted upon staying on the walls all night to encourage his men. He had a relapse next morning, and within a day or two he was dead, worn out by distemper and fatigue. He was a victim to his unfailing devotion to duty. Walker, Mitchelburne and four colonels were pallbearers at his funeral. He was buried in the north aisle of the cathedral where he lies to this day. Seth Whittle, Rector of Ballyskulliary, preached the sermon, who himself was to be dead before the end of the siege.

There was much jealous backbiting amongst the leaders of the garrison, but no man uttered a word of criticism against Henry Baker. Walker, all careful to gain credit for himself during conflicts in the siege, paid a generous tribute to Baker, saying that his death was a great loss to the garrison and generally lamented. He said that Baker was a valiant person; in all his actions he showed great honour, courage and conduct, and that he might be able to write a great account of his character. Mackenzie refers to Baker's prudent and resolute conduct and to the affection in which he was held by the people of Londonderry. He was 'greatly beloved and very well qualified for the government, being endued with great patience and moderation, free from envy or malice'. Mitchelburne, whom Baker wounded in a duel and whom he had confined to quarters, spoke of him as 'our noble brave Governor' and said that his bravery should never be forgotten. The poet Aicken wrote that:—

A funeral sermon's preached, the bells did ring,
And treble volleys did his praises sing.

William III later presented a coat of arms to Baker's son with the motto of 'No Surrender'. The crest is a Londonderry bastion surmounted by a marbled fist holding a loaf of bread, which the citizens had defiantly thrown at the Catholics. The bread above the bastion is a pun on Baker's name. When Baker was already a sick man, the Council had asked him to name a deputy, and without hesitation he had pointed to Mitchelburne, who, as we have seen, he imprisoned.

Ash said that no malice burned in Baker's mind against Mitchelburne, though there had been a difference between them. Mitchelburne was therefore released from custody so that he could help organize the defence, and upon Baker's death he was confirmed in his appointment. Walker implies to his account of the siege that he himself had become sole Governor upon Baker's death. However there is no doubt that documents were signed by both Walker and Mitchelburne as joint Governors, and that the contemporaries regarded Mitchelburne as Walker's equal. Mitchelburne told the House of Commons some years later that he had been chosen as Governor and Commander in Chief along with Dr Walker. He performed all the duties Walker performed, having full charge of the military part of the siege.

Baker had made a good choice; Mitchelburne, a man of forty-three, was the most experienced soldier in the garrison. He had been commissioned in Charles II's time, and he had served in James's Irish army and then, like Baker, had come north to fight for the Protestant cause. He was commissioned by William of Orange. He is best remembered as the man who flew a crimson flag from the cathedral steeple, which became known as 'Mitchelburne's bloody flag', symbol of Londonderry today, and to this day at least one Orange Lodge bears the name 'Crimson Defenders'. At this point the garrison needed resolute leadership, for Hamilton and Rosen were now trying new measures to effect the surrender which their king wanted. Hamilton thought that it was best to make an appeal directly to the people of Londonderry, bypassing the leadership. To this end, a letter was fired in an empty bomb over the walls. He was well aware that Rosen was feared by the citizens, and he assured them in the letter that he — Hamilton — would be responsible for making terms. He said that those who decided to remain in the city and who would swear allegiance to King James, would be given protection and free liberty of goods and religion. Those who wished to return to their homes would be escorted there under a safe conduct; they would be supplied with food, given back their property and awarded compensation for their cattle that might have been taken to the mountains.

Copies of the proposal, says Walker, were distributed in the town by villains, but all to no purpose. Mackenzie said that Hamilton was mistaken in thinking that the people might be more amenable than the officers and leaders. It was the rank and file that had adamantly cried "No Surrender!" at an earlier date. The leadership, more aware of the perilous state of the town than the people, were always more willing to negotiate. It was put about in Londonderry that it would cost a man his life if any one thought about surrender.

The Council delayed in their reply to the Catholic overtures, and were busy sizing up the state of the garrison, which now was reduced to feeding on horse flesh, dogs, cats, rats and mice, and greaves of a year old. They had plenty of tallows and starch, as well as salted and dried hides. They unanimously agreed that they would eat the Catholics or themselves rather than surrender to the enemy. Their reply pointed out that Londonderry would put no faith in General Hamilton's promises. They pointed out that they once trusted him, but trusted him no more, for he had unworthily broken faith with William. Although Hamilton had promised that Rosen would have no power to interfere, Rosen did so. On 30th June, showing some of the ruthlessness he had learnt in the Thirty Years' War, he sent Londonderry an ultimatum. He gave them until six o'clock on the following evening to surrender, failing which he would round up all the Protestants in the neighbourhood, all those related to the people behind the gates, and drive them under the walls. He said that the people of Londonderry would be allowed to open their gates to them and let them into the city; otherwise they would be forced to see their friends and relations starve in front of them. Orders had already been issued to commanders at Coleraine, Antrim, Carrickfergus, Belfast, Dungannon, Charlemont, Belturbet, Sligo, Ballyshannon, the Finnwater and the neighbourhood of Dungannon.

Rosen also said that he would lay waste the countryside, so that if help did arrive from England, the soldiers would be starved through lack of sustenance. Rosen said that this was the Protestants' last chance. If the city was obstinate, then neither age nor sex would be spared.

The Protestants did not believe that Rosen would carry out his threat. On July 2nd, Walker and Mitchelburne, the ultimatum having expired, made their reply to Hamilton; the reply had been delayed because of Baker's death. They said that the Catholics' brutal strength gave great offence to the garrison, and that they did not believe that Hamilton or Rosen would keep their promises made at an earlier date. They said they expected favours from King James and General Hamilton. They said that they did not trust Rosen or his countrymen. The Governors, it would appear, were genuinely willing to come to terms. However, it is difficult to make out whether they were trying to play off Hamilton against Rosen, or whether they were just procrastinating. The last seems the most likely explanation. They said that the commission by which James had authorized Hamilton to make terms was dated 1st May. Since that date a parliament had sat in Dublin, confiscating all their estates. The garrison requested Hamilton to obtain a further commission to treat with us.

James was bound to a promise that whatever terms they might agree with Hamilton would be fulfilled, so that it would not be in the power of Rosen or any Frenchman to break what articles shall be made for our advantage. Rosen made good his promise before Hamilton could reply. On 2nd July the Protestants were driven under the walls, and they were under great distress, all the men, women and children. Many, mainly women, perished en route to Londonderry. They had been stripped and put for the night into cattle pounds and dilapidated houses. The first wave of refugees were about 200 strong. They approached the walls, but the garrison thought it was a Catholic attack and opened fire on them, but fortunately they only hit three of the Catholic soldiers who were driving the Protestants to the walls.

Many of the Catholic officers considered it a barbaric task and they were in tears as they drove them forth. A thousand more Protestants were herded to the walls the next morning, and they told the Protestants in the city not to admit them or yield to the Catholics, saying that if the city surrendered they would all be put to death. They were then driven from the walls to spend the night at Windmill Hill. The garrison had managed to take the most useful of the Protestants into the city. The Protestants attempted to send back 500 of their more useful brethren and turned back all the men they came across, picking them out by their ragged clothes, their gaunt appearance and in some cases by their unpleasant smell.

The answer to Rosen's policies was that the garrison, warmed with rage and fury against the Catholics, erected a large gallows at the Double Bastion, in full view of the Catholics. The garrison let it be known that if the Catholics did not let all the Protestants return to their homes without being harmed, then they would bring their Catholic prisoners in Londonderry in full sight of their friends. The Protestants informed the Catholics that priests might enter the city in order to prepare the prisoners for death; however no priests came, and it was left up to Lieutenant Colonel Campbell and Christopher Jenny, a clergyman, to prepare the Catholics for death. The Catholics accepted the verdict with resignation, and said that they would not blame the Protestants for taking their lives in view of the Catholic policies towards the victims under the walls. They were allowed to make one last appeal to Hamilton. They said that they — the Catholics — were all condemned to die tomorrow unless Rosen and Hamilton changed their policies. They had incensed the Governors of Londonderry by their attitude. They had received no answer from Rosen despite having sent him a communication. They now requested that Hamilton represent their conditions to Rosen, for the lives of twenty prisoners were at stake. Furthermore they said that they were all willing to die for His Majesty, and that they could not blame the garrison for shedding their blood. They said that the Governors had treated them well and with every civility. To show his great regard for his friends, Hamilton sent a heartlessly curt reply:– He said that it was the prisoners' fault that they were going to die, but that their death would be avenged when the Catholic army entered the city. It was signed 'Yours — R Hamilton'.

A day or two later the Catholics were released from their ordeal under the walls and were allowed to return to their houses. Likewise the Catholic prisoners in the city were allowed to return to their quarters. The garrison made an attempt to smuggle out some of their sick and womenfolk with the refugees, but so lean did the Protestants look, that the Catholics were able to recognise them immediately and did not let them go. Ash speculated that if the Catholics released the Protestants, then they knew that they were going to hang their Protestant prisoners. But Hamilton's heart was never in the business, and when the Protestants had at first been driven through the Catholic camp, he gave them food in defiance of Rosen's orders.

There were Protestant Jacobites in the Irish ranks, who were enraged at Rosen's barbarous treatment of the prisoners. Rosen told James that he had never really intended that the Protestants should be starved to death, and that he was only using it as a ploy to get the city to surrender. James was in a rage when he heard about Rosen's behaviour, and told Lord Granard that none but a barbarous Muscovite could conceive such a policy. Avaux, backing Rosen's actions, said that the king's annoyance sprang from the fact that he was not consulted in advance. Melfort commented that if Rosen had been a British subject, he would have been hanged. When the Bishop of Meath hurried to plead with James to exercise clemency, he found that his representations were unnecessary. The king told the bishop that he had already sent word to countermand Rosen's orders. But he pointed out that Rosen was a foreigner and that such barbarous behaviour might be acceptable to a Russian, but that if Rosen had been a British subject, he would have called him to account for it.

The Marshal General could only receive a rebuke from James. He told the bishop that he had sent the Protestants back to their quarters without injury to their persons. James comes out of the incident with full marks, and it seems that it was his intervention that saved the Protestants according to some historians. But the fact is that Rosen had countermanded the orders keeping the Protestants under the walls after Rosen had changed his mind. Milligan states that it was

J

the Protestants' threat of retaliation that saved the Catholic prisoners and the Protestants under the walls.

Kirke was still lying in Lough Foyle and he had already passed on a message from William and Mary that any barbarous behaviour towards Protestants would bring retaliation from England: 'The King doth think himself obliged to return in the same manner upon all Papists of what rank or consideration so ever that shall be found here, and he will not fail to put this in execution according to the provocation given'. On 2nd July, Kirke issued a proclamation addressed to 'the General of the Irish Forces', in which he said that Rosen's behaviour was unjustified and unchristian, and this came well from the butcher of Sedgemoor. James, however, had already made moves for Rosen's recall. James made representations to the French court to get Rosen replaced in view of his actions at Londonderry. These representations were made through Lord Dover, and James decried Rosen's action of driving the Protestants under the walls. He said that no promises would be believed given by Rosen, nor indeed from any of his officers, until the truth about the affair was known by way of the Protestants. He said that some Protestants in Ulster were running to Enniskillen for protection against Rosen.

Rosen himself was glad enough to be recalled and said that there was little glory to be had at Londonderry. A few days earlier he had sent James a long letter of complaints.

He said that Kirke was always at his post, and awaiting reinforcements from England — three regiments of cavalry and two of infantry, believed to be under command of the formidable Schomberg. As far as the Catholics were concerned, the reinforcements that were being sent up from Dublin would be useless, for the greater part of the arms they were carrying were broken, and there was not in all the Catholic army a gunsmith to mend them. Avaux had reported that in all his regiments they have but seven muskets, and the rest have sticks. Some had pikes which were not shod with iron.

Rosen stated that the troops Hamilton had with him at Londonderry were in an even worse state. There was not a battalion with more than 200 men, with more than two-thirds of them without swords, belts or bandoliers. The cruel Ulster weather had taken its toll, and deaths happened fast in the Catholic camp; they had nothing to live on except oatmeal, water, with some raw lean beef. Rosen had expressed his amazement that Walter Butler's regiment had been sent up from Dublin without sword, powder or ball. Bagenal's regiment had been sent forth without ammunition. It was responsible for carrying the troops' money. He criticized the Quartermaster General's Department, saying that no one was worried about the state of the troops.

Rosen stayed on at Londonderry for two or three weeks, sulking in his tent, and he dissociated himself from the conduct of the siege. He declared that he was always against the besieging of the city, and that his advice had been ignored. Rosen's departure from Londonderry was regretted by no one. No one could endure him and he eventually departed for France. However Louis XIV still remembered his friend and made him a Marshal of France. At about this time, James procured the recall of Avaux. It was said that Avaux was a man of common sense who had obtained a good reputation from the different embassies he was in. James had become discontented with Avaux's arrogant and disrespectful manner; he had a sharp tongue and a highly critical approach.

Chapter 20

"No Surrender!"

Dundee wanted more help from Scotland for Ireland, and James was more than ever set to get the citizens of Londonderry to surrender, so that he might join his loyal Highlanders. On 5th July, James gave his men authority to treat with the men of Londonderry on whatever terms they liked. On the same day he told Hamilton that he was to be as conservative as possible. He was told to offer them their lives, fortunes, a royal pardon for all that is past, and protection.

Surrender at this point may have been possible, for starvation was now playing havoc with the garrison. They were so bad that they had to kill a horse grazing near the Windmill. Despair was everywhere, for Kirke was not making a move. Mackenzie says that when the Derry men saw the fleet in the lough not making an attempt to come up, it cast a cold shadow over their hopes. The defenders might have been willing to listen to any useful proposals, but Rosen's behaviour had now raised the old cry of "No Surrender!" The Protestants distrusted the Catholic's good faith. An appeal was launched to the soldiers and citizens on 10th July by Hamilton over the leaders' heads by firing a 'dead shell' into the city; this landed in the graveyard of the cathedral, and it can be seen in the porch to this day. It has the inscription that 'This shell was thrown into the city by the besieging army and containing proposals for a surrender'. Is was addressed to the soldiers and inhabitants of Derry. It said that the conditions laid down by Lieutenant General Hamilton were sincere. The power he had over the king was real, for he was no longer influenced by the likes of Rosen. They were not to be ignorant of the king's clemency towards his subjects. If the citizens surrendered, their religion would be respected, and if any wanted to leave the kingdom then they would have passes. The Protestants would have their estates returned and have liberty of religion, whatever it be.

If they doubted the powers given to General Hamilton by James, twenty of them were invited to see the patent, with freedom under the king's hand and seal. They were not to be obstinate against their natural prince. The privations which the citizens were undergoing were unnecessary, which would grow worse and worse if they continued to rebel, for they would be too late in surrendering if they did not take up the present offer of clemency.

The citizens were tempted to respond to these proposals for conditions within the city were becoming more and more desperate. Walker noted that the garrison's fighting strength was dwindling. From 750 at the start of the siege to 5,520 on 8th July, 4,892 on 25th and 4,456 on 27th. There was only one end to such progression. He compiled a shopping list, an account given by a gentleman who took care of the food:– Horse flesh: 1/8 a lb. Quarter of a dog 5/6 (fattened by eating the bodies of the slain Irish). A dog's head: 2/6. A cat: 4/6. A rat: 1/0. A mouse 6d. A small flock taken in the river: Not to be bought for money or purchased under the rate of a quantity of meal. Greaves, tallow, salted hides: 1/0, 4/0, 1/0 a lb respectively. A quart of horse blood: 1/0. A horse pudding 6d. A handful of sea starch: 2d or chickweed 1d. A quart of meal, when found: 1/0.

The garrison's rations went down as quickly as its fighting strength. By July it was a far cry from the carefree days of April when a man's weekly allowance had been four pounds of beef, four quarts of meal and three pounds of salmon. Salmon did not appear on the menu until 15th May, when some officers of 'Mountro's' regiment received three pounds a piece. A form of coarse oatmeal called 'shilling' was in use by 1st June. In that month there was no beef at all until 25th, when each man got half a pound, supplemented by tallow at the rate of a pound a man.

There was a good stock of spices in Londonderry, and in the first week of July each man was issued with two pounds of ginger and two pounds of aniseed with which to flavour the tasteless shilling and tallow. A large store of starch was discovered by a man called Cunningham. Ash says that it was a new diet for the men, and that it was called Dutch flour, made into pancakes. Mackenzie says that the pancakes were made by mixing starch and tallow, and that this proved to be good food. Walker agrees that this diet of starch and tallow nourished the garrison, and that it was a great cure for the distemper and preserved others from it. The discovery of starch only tied the garrison over for a week, and then, as Walker stated they would have to take to cannibalism.

There now appears a fat man upon the scene, and he makes a brief appearance only in the pages of the historians. He hid himself for three days, since he thought the garrison might eat him. John Hunter of Maghera remembered how his face had blackened with hunger, and how he had been so weak that he had fallen under his musket as he was going to his station on the walls. He said that God gave him strength to stay at his post all night and enabled him to play the part of the soldier as strong as he ever was. There was no clean water, and he suffered severely from thirst. He was so famished that he would have eaten any lice he could have laid his hand upon. It was unbelievable, so one John Hunter stated, what people suffered in the siege. Those that had been careful about their food before it, would now eat anything — a dog or a cat or a mouse. The famine was so great that many a man, woman or child, died from want of food. A pound of oatmeal and a pound of tallow had to last a man a week, and sometimes there were salt hides — according to George Holmes, writing from Strabane to a friend in Cumberland. He said that it was as bad as Samaria and that they had only pigeons' dung.

On 12th July, in the morning, the citizens of Lough Foyle looked down the lough to see that most of the English ships had disappeared overnight. The garrison did not know where they had gone said Mackenzie; for all the people of Londonderry knew, they might have lost heart and returned to England. It was decided to negotiate once again with Hamilton, and six commissioners were appointed for this purpose — Colonels Lance and Hugh Hamill; Captains White and Dobbin; Alderman Cocken, who was now a Captain; and the Chaplain of Walker's regiment, Reverend John Mackenzie. Their authority came from the leaders, soldiers and citizens of Londonderry. Thirty-four signatures were attached, amongst them those of Walker, Mitchelburne, Adam Murray and Captain Ash. The terms which they were to reach had been given to them by Hamilton from which they could not deviate. Anyone else that had borne arms against King James in Ulster and Connaught — including everyone in Londonderry — was to receive a royal pardon and was to have his lands and personal property restored to him. All Protestants were to have freedom of religion, and the clergy in the two provinces were to be given back their churches and titles. If anyone in Londonderry wished to go to Scotland or England he was free to do so. No one was obliged to take an oath of allegiance to James or to be made to enter his service. Officers and gentlemen were permitted to retain one servant each and to keep and wear their swords. The Catholic pikemen and the mobs in Ulster and Connaught were to be disarmed and prevented from killing Protestants, or from roving around the country. Any troops in Londonderry that wished to go down to Culmore, by land or sea to join the English ships, were free to do so. They would be allowed to march out of Londonderry with all the honours of war, drums beating, colours flying, their matches alight and their weapons in their hands. The terms had to be confirmed by 26th July either by an act of the Irish Parliament or by the king under the Great Seal of Ireland. Commissioners were to be appointed so that the terms were kept in the two provinces and in Londonderry.

Hostages meanwhile were to be given by both sides; Hamilton's would be kept on the English ships and the Protestants in one of the Catholic camps at Londonderry. If the city was relieved by July, all would be released. Until this date there was to be an armistice. If Londonderry were relieved, then the terms would cease to be binding on either side. In return for accepting this long list of demands, the garrison would surrender on 26th July to Hamilton, with all its stores, armaments and ammunition. On the 13th July, armed with these proposals, they met their opposite numbers on the strand; they were escorted to a special tent, where they were wined and dined before getting down to business. The arguments continued well into the night, and Hamilton, had not forgotten James's instructions to secure the surrender of the town at any cost. He went as far as he was able to secure the garrison's co-operation. There were three arguments that he could not agree with. First, he could not agree with a date as far ahead as the 26th; if Londonderry was to surrender, it must do so as early as noon on 15th, only two days away. Secondly, he insisted that his own hostages be kept in the city and not put aboard the English ships. Thirdly, if and when the garrison marched out, only the officers and gentlemen could bear arms, not the rank and file.

Hamilton's insistence upon an early date for surrender is understandable. One also wonders why he was so insistent upon the location of the hostages and the protocol of the march out. The garrison were pitching their demands high in the hope that they could bluff out until Kirke arrived back in the Foyle. Avaux was quite certain that this was their intention; he reported to James that the Protestants had provided themselves with fresh water and had laughed at him for sending extravagant proposals. Avaux warned James that unless there was positive action, he would lose all his army before Count Solmes, one of William's leading generals, arrived in Ireland. Negotiations were not at a deadlock, but the garrison's commissioners were allowed to return to Londonderry. They were given until noon the following day to provide an answer for the points at issue, but the Council in Londonderry were only willing to give way on one of them. They agreed to leave the manner of the march out up to both commissioners, but they firmly said that there would be no surrender before 26th July; further that the Catholic hostages must be lodged on the English ships. The garrison's insistence upon the disputed terms was clearly dependent upon their distrust of the Catholics, for the Irish Parliament would not be able to ratify the terms within two days. At this negotiations ended and hostilities resumed.

While the garrison was busy negotiating, they had at last found out what Kirke was doing. The disappearance of a large part of his fleet from Lough Foyle, did not mean that the Major General had deserted them. He had in fact launched a diversionary expedition to Inch Island at the head of Lough Swilly. In doing this he denied the enemy a fertile island abounding in grain, from which the Catholics were drawing most of their supplies at Inch Island. Kirke's men would have an opportunity of stretching their legs, after having been cooped up aboard ship.

On 7th July, a force of 600 men were sent under command of Colonel Steuart to the Foyle, where they anchored off Rathmullan. The Duke of Berwick, with his 1,500 horse and foot, had quickly tried the patience of the British infantry, and he would make little progress against the cannon fire of the English frigates lying off Rathmullan. News of the small expedition to Inch Island reached Londonderry through a small boy, who brought two despatches for them from the Major General. He brought the message in a letter concealed in his garter, and the second one was hidden by running it up the boy's bum. In the latter letter, Walker and Mitchleburne informed Kirke that they had only food supplies left for another five days. They said that above 5,000 men were already dead from want of sustenance and that those that survived had hardly the energy to make it to the walls. Here many of them died nightly at their posts. They said that they had been offered very generous terms from the enemy, which they rejected with the hope of relief from the sea. The Catholics, they said, vowed neither to spare age nor sex. They could not understand why Kirke had not attempted a relief, for the wind was favourable many times. They said that the boom across the River Foyle was broken, so that ships might easily pass. In actual fact the idea that the boom was broken was a fallacy.

Kirke sent the young boy back to Londonderry with another message, this time hidden in his breeches, and not his backside. It said that Kirke had received the garrison's letters by way of Inch Island, saying that he had written to them on a Sunday and that he was doing everything possible for their relief, but that he had found it impossible by the river. Kirke said that he was causing a diversion at Inch Island, so that he could relieve the Protestants. He said that he had sent officers, ammunition, arms and great guns to Enniskillen, where there were 3,000 foot and 1,500 horses and a regiment of dragoons that had promised to come to their relief. He said that he would attack the enemy via Inch Island. He was expecting 6,000 men from England at any minute. There were stores and provisions, and he was determined to relieve them. Everything was going fine in Scotland and England, he said. He described the Catholics as a 'barbarous people'.

The garrison was to let Kirke know about the state of affairs as often as possible. He said that several of the enemy had deserted to him, and he was learning about the state of affairs in the Catholic camp. Apparently the Catholics could not stay very long at Londonderry. He had heard word from Enniskillen that the Duke of Berwick was beaten.

The young boy that had carried the letter, was sent back to Londonderry with another message, but this time he fell into the hands of the enemy. Luckily he swallowed the message that he was carrying and resisted all attempts by the Catholics to get information out of him. He managed to escape and get back to Kirke, where he was awarded an ensign's commission on the spot. The name of this young boy is lost to history.

Another means of finding out the position of the Protestants, was via a man who lived at Whitecastle, situated on the Donegal side of Lough Foyle. There was a certain stone ashore, said Captain Richards, under which he put letters, and he made signs to the Catholics to come and fetch the letters. He and his wife, covered in a white mantle, walked backwards and forwards on the beach and so returned to their house again, which was a sign for the Catholics to come and fetch the letters. At dusk on a Summer's evening, two white figures could be seen pacing the shore on their lonely vigil. Kirke's second letter reached Walker while Mackenzie and his fellow commissioners were still negotiating with the Catholics. Walker had it copied out for general circulation and embellished it with a statement which did not appear in the original. The letter stated that Kirke had sent 1,000 foot and 9,000 horse to Inch. When Mackenzie and his commissioners returned from their first negotiations to report Hamilton's counter-demands, it was Walker who urged that the terms be accepted and that the city should be surrendered the following day. Walker was told that it was no time to be talking about surrender. Word came that a relieving force had landed at Inch; Walker, according to Mackenzie confessed that part of the letter had been written by himself. Ash, also, records the arrival of a letter, saying that 12,000 men were landed in Lough Swilly and that 2,000 horse had gone round there also. Walker seems to have exaggerated the number of men landed at Inch Island, and he seems to have done this to keep up the garrison's morale. It seems strange that Walker should have come down in favour of an immediate surrender. Only the day before he had written to Kirke saying that the city could not hold out for more than fourteen days. Kirke hoped that before this time he would be able to relieve them. Walker may have found Hamilton's counter-proposals attractive and that they should be accepted immediately.

It was inevitable that from time to time someone like Walker should attract criticism from the hard-pressed garrison, and he had been warned from the Catholic camp that there might be those out to discredit him. There was a rumour spreading through the garrison that there was a danger of mutiny and that he had in store a huge private stock of food. It was suggested that his house should be searched, and Walker complying, the soldiers returned to a good opinion of their Governor. A rumour was also spread abroad from the Catholic camp that he was planning to betray the town and was going to be richly rewarded for having done so. The first that Walker knew of this was when some members of the garrison grew cautious. He traced the story back to a certain Mr Cole, who had been captured by the Catholics and interrogated by Richard Hamilton. Hamilton inquired what sort of person Walker was, and who he knew. Cole replied that he was intimate with himself, hoping to regain his liberty. It was hoped that Walker could be lured away from the Protestant cause. However Walker ordered Cole to be detained once he had tracked down the source of the rumour. Upon being questioned Cole cleared Walker's name, and the Governor was back in the garrison's confidence.

It is not clear if Walker recommended the immediate surrender of the town on 15th July; but the majority of the garrison's leaders came out strongly for holding out. The state of affairs was now becoming desperate. The garrison now, on 26th July, tried to replenish their stock of food, and their spirits had been roused by a stirring address by Walker. He said that the Catholics boasted of their number and strength. But they said that they had God on their side, for with only a small force in Londonderry, the garrison held out against the enemy. They had looked Rosen in the face and broken their boats and idols. Their bombs did not frighten the garrison, and their consciences were clear about what they were doing. They thought God Almighty would defend them, and they were to keep up their spirits, if they had any care for their estates, wives and children. They were hated and persecuted chiefly because of their religion, and it would be for this glory that they would hold out. They would defend Londonderry to the last drop of Protestant blood. Walker raised his voice at this point in a thunderous "So Help Us God!" All the garrison cried a great "Amen". These were not the words of a man that had been urging an imminent surrender. Walker was truly the progenitor of that line of clergymen like Roaring Hanna and Dr Ian Paisley. Walker delivered another sermon, the one he had been giving just over. This time it was addressed to the 400 men who were to take part in the following sortie. He appealed to the men, telling them what would happen to them if James succeeded in taking Londonderry. He warned the men that the priests would be triumphant and that the Popish principles would prevail everywhere. Their wives and children would be at the mercy of the Catholic dragoons. Their houses would be plundered and people slaughtered. Fire would rage in the streets. He said that the people of Londonderry should rather die than be victims of Catholicism. It was better to perish in a religious cause than live under James.

On 26th July, at three o'clock in the morning, Walker's men, now sworn to secrecy, crept out of Bishop's Gate trying to capture some cattle which the Catholics were grazing close to the walls. The Catholics were taken completely by surprise, and although one Catholic regiment promptly formed up in good order, only three musketeers had their matches alight. Walker says that they came across the Catholics near Butcher's Gate, and killed 300 of their men, besides officers. Many of the Protestants could not pursue the Catholics since they were weak with hunger, and many of them fell with their own blows. The raiding party returned without having captured any cattle, and now the garrison was forced to rely upon one remaining ploy, using one of their last remaining cows. They tied the cow at a stake and set fire to her. They were counting that the screams of the cow would induce the Catholics' cattle to come to her assistance, whose tails at the noise, were already lifted up. The stratagem did not work, for the cow got loose. With the failure to replenish their meat supplies, the garrison was very near the end, but they still felt it their duty to hold out. John Hunter recalled that "I was so hard put to it, by reason of the want of food, that I had hardly heart to speak or walk; and yet when the enemy was coming, as many a time they did to storm the walls, then I found as if my former strength returned to me. I am sure it was the Lord that kept the city and more else; for there were many of us that could hardly stand on our feet before the enemy attacked the walls who, when they were assaulting the out-trenches, ran out against the most nimbly and with great courage".

The garrison did not realize that the Catholics were in as almost a bad state. About 20th July, John Hamilton had reported to James that at the start of the siege he had fourteen battalions under his command. The Catholic battalion had been 600 strong as opposed to the Catholic strength of 5,000 men. By now the numbers behind the walls had been diminished by sickness and mortality, and Hamilton's army had been reduced sadly by deaths, wounds, sickness and desertion. Rosen was being of no help, keeping to his bed and resolved not to meddle. If something was not done quickly Hamilton's men would soon be starving, for everything was quite bare around Londonderry.

Hamilton's report crossed with a letter from James in which the king once more reiterated his desire that Londonderry would be captured before it was relieved. It was essential that the matter should be resolved as soon as possible, and he said that men's lives must inevitably be lost in the enterprise. Eggs had to be broken in order to make an omelette. Hamilton had anticipated which line the king would take, and had already canvassed the views of his fellow officers at a Council of War. All had agreed that the shortage of ammunition, guns and men, made it impossible to storm Londonderry; the best plan was to starve the city into surrender, which could only be done if the besiegers had the time and troops to bring about an assault. It was necessary to prevent Kirke from relieving Londonderry by sea.

Berwick had the view that it was impossible to take the town by storm with the little number of foot they had or without a large number of battery guns. He said that "Unless they want provisions they will never surrender". Hamilton agreed with his Generals and fowarded their collective opinion to Dublin, and James relied heavily upon their opinion, which he respected. He accepted their view that the only way was to starve the city into surrender. James wrote to Hamilton that seeing that Londonderry would not be taken by force by the small number of troops upon the spot, it was best to follow their advice and force the city into a surrender by starvation.

As we have seen, a diversionary expedition had been sent to Inch Island. On 7th July, Steuart and his 600 men had landed there. A fortnight later they had a fleeting visit from Kirke, who sailed back to Lough Foyle on the same evening. On 12th July, the *James* of Londonderry, a little ship that had been taken by the French and then retaken by the British, came sailing up the Swilly with fresh orders from Kirke. Steuart's little force had now been reinforced by thousands of Protestants who had headed to Inch. He read with dismay that Kirke, after a reconnaissance, had concluded that Inch Island would be indefensible in the face of the Catholic artillery. Rather than be driven out in confusion it would be better to conclude a hasty retreat. He ordered that the 600 regulars whom Steuart had brought with him as distinct from the new men, the local Protestants who had enlisted at Inch, should immediately be re-embarked on the transports.

Steuart had the strong support of Captain Richards, along with the Council of War. He took it upon himself to reply that he was not willing to carry out Kirke's orders, unless they were confirmed after his arguments against them had been considered. His position was now strongly fortified, and he said that he had sixteen cannon dug into emplacements on the shore. Ten more cannon would give covering power from the two warships that remained in Lough Swilly. He did not believe that the Catholics would attack him as long as Londonderry held out, and he then heard the news from Dr Leslie that the Catholics were deserting daily in fear of an attack from Enniskillen.

But what happened to those Protestants who had taken refuge on Inch Island, and was Kirke going to abandon them to their fate? About 12,000 Protestants had fled to Inch, and they could not expect mercy at Catholic hands. Meanwhile events were moving fast at Londonderry, now bringing matters to a climax. Kirke was now prodded into action by Schomberg, to carry out the task for which he had been chosen — and that was to relieve Londonderry.

Chapter 21

The Boom is Broken

Schomberg was both a Marshal of France and a Duke of England, and it was he that persuaded Kirke to relieve Londonderry. He was born in Heidelberg, Friedrich Herman Schomberg in 1615, and he was now in his seventies. He had been a professional soldier all his life, having served in Holland, Sweden and France. He was made a Marshal of France in 1675. He was a Protestant, and upon the revocation of the Edict of Nantes in 1685, left France to enter the service of the Elector of Brandenburg. In 1688, with the elector's consent, he had joined William of Orange as 'second in command' of the expedition to England. He was made a Knight of the Garter, a baron, a marquis and a duke as well as being made Master General of the Ordnance. He was therefore a man of vast experience and had a personal interest in Londonderry where his son was a soldier behind the walls. Walker called him 'Captain Schambroom'.

On 3rd July, he wrote to Kirke from Whitehall, saying that the excuse given by the Major General's Council of War for not attempting the relief of the city was that he was not certain whether the boom and chain across the Foyle could be broken or that he could sail across the boats that had been sunk in the river. Kirke was ordered to ascertain the situation by sending reconnaissance officers to view the places and to size up the situation for themselves. It was essential that they should be able to break the boom and chain in order to relieve the town.

Faced with these orders, Kirke could procrastinate no longer. He ordered three ships to be laden with provisions, with forty musketeers to each ship. These three being merchantmen, were the *Phoenix* of Coleraine, a 50-ton vessel commanded by a Glaswegian, Captain Reynell, and the *Mountjoy* of Londonderry, of about 130 tons — the ship that broke the boom and saved the Apprentice Boys. The captain of the *Mountjoy* was Micaiah or Michael Browning, who was a native of Londonderry, and he had been one of the most rigorous protesters against Kirke's inactivity. These three ships were to be escorted by 'Their Majesties' Ship' *Dartmouth*, commanded by the intrepid Leake.

There was only one other warship in the lough at this time, the *Swallow*; she was too large to make the river passage and Leake borrowed her longboat and together with nine seamen, he helped to hack his way through the boom. The task confronting Leake's flotilla was daunting. The ships had first to pass Culmore, with the Catholic guns blazing at them. After this they had to sail the four miles upstream in a channel which had deeply shelving banks and which was too narrow. Above Culmore lay two more forts, on the starboard quarter, Newfort, which lay midway between Culmore and the boom. The second was Charlesfort, which overlooked the boom itself, while to port there was a fourth strong point called Grangefort. Irish infantry lined both banks; there was horse and dragoons entrenched, ready to open up fire along with the musketry. If the little ship managed to pass by the Catholic guns, there remained the problem of breaking the boom.

The boom was 200 yards long at a point where the Foyle was 700 feet wide at low tide, and 1,400 feet wide at high tide. Pointis was convinced that his boom would be a formidable obstacle for the English ships. However there was a shortage of artillery on the Catholic side, and the artillerymen, as James had noted, were not the best.

Leake and his merchantmen were now aware that it was essential to spring into action if the city had to avoid a surrender to the Catholics. Mitchelburne's bloody crimson red flag had already been flown several times to let Kirke know of their position. Eight shots had been fired from the steeple for the same purpose. Six great guns were fired by the fleet in reply, which the garrison interpreted as letting them know that the ships were going to relieve the city at high tide. Meanwhile Leake had been concerting his plans with the captain of the three ships: The *Dartmouth* would lead the *Mountjoy* and the *Phoenix* as far as Culmore. Here they would engage the fort's batteries, so that they would sail safely into the River Foyle. Now would follow the task of breaking the boom by ramming it. The crew of the *Swallow*'s longboat assisted them with their axes and helped to haul the ships through the boom. The *Jerusalem* was kept in reserve, and she was not to make a move until the other ships were safely through the obstacle.

On 28th July, *Dartmouth* got underway. It was about seven o'clock on a calm Sunday Summer evening. She made course for Culmore, and was followed by *Mountjoy*, *Phoenix* and the longboat. This move had not gone unnoticed by the starving citizens on the walls. Walker had given them a rousing address, and records that about an hour after the sermon they saw some ships come up the lough, and they interpreted this as meaning that Kirke was now in a position to relieve them and was carrying out his promise. The guns at Culmore blazed away at the *Dartmouth* as soon as she came within range. Captain Leake, according to the *London Gazette*, behaved very bravely.

Under cover of the *Dartmouth*'s guns, the two victualling ships made their way past Culmore. After this the *Dartmouth* dropped anchor, having neutralized the fort and having battered the upper part of the wall down, leaving the Catholics without shelter.

By six o'clock that evening the wind had been blowing a moderate gale, but it dropped to a dead calm by the time they made Culmore. There was only the

141

flood tide to carry the victualling ships towards the boom.

As they made their way upstream, the Catholics fired heavily upon them. *Mountjoy*, the heavier vessel, rammed the boom and broke the iron part of it, while the crew of the longboat chopped at the wooden part of the boom with their axes, a task which they easily achieved, so much so, that the Catholics thought that it was done by some kind of magic. An account in a journal from London said that 'some say there went first a boat with a house upon it (the longboat) and came to the boom . . . and of a sudden a man (a witch they say) struck three stakes with a hatchet upon the boom and cut it asunder, and so passed on; and then the ships followed'.

Avaux of course did not believe in witchcraft; he thought that it merely proved the inefficiency of Pointis. The boom had been badly constructed, so he reported to James a few days later. However the *Mountjoy* was in trouble, for after her collision with the boom, she had rebounded unto a mud bank on the right shore. The Catholics yelled in triumph, and made ready to board her, whilst the citizens of Londonderry's hearts sank at hearing the shouts. They had been anxiously straining their eyes through the gathering dusk of the Summer evening. Their hopes expired, said Mackenzie, whilst Macaulay said that they looked at each other with fear in their eyes.

Walker said that the Catholic cheers were the loudest that the people had experienced. Two regiments of Catholic horse rode into the shallows to capture the *Mountjoy*. Captain Browning, sword in hand, stood on the deck. He cheered on his men. The *Mountjoy* let fly with three guns, at which the Catholics fled.

The French general was angry with his men for running away, and used all means to make them attack the Protestant ship again, but the soldiers refused. If the Irish artillerymen had been efficient, the boom would never have been broken. Nicolas Plunkett in *Light to the Blind* stated:– 'Lord, who see'est the hearts of people, we leave the judgement of this affair to thy mercy in the interim those gunners lost Ireland'.

The blast from the *Mountjoy*'s guns had not only scattered the Catholics, but the rebound shifted her off the mud and sent her lurching back into deep water.

Led by *Phoenix*, she made her way through the boom, the two little ships making their way down the Foyle to Londonderry. The wind was not blowing as freshly as when they had set sail. The *Mountjoy* was towed upstream by the longboat, and from Pennyburn onwards the people of Derry came out to tow the ships in. It is puzzling where the garrison got the boats from, since previously they had to make an eight-oared vessel. The people made their way down to the Ship Quay with empty casks and hogsheads, which they filled with earth, to protect them against enemy fire, whilst the food was brought in.

It was now ten o'clock at night and almost dark. The ships were tied up and the stores and food brought into the city. There were good things aboard ship for the citizens. There was meal, great cheeses, casks of beef, bacon, butter, pease and biscuit, brandy. Not long before the people had been on a starvation diet. The rations which each now received was three pounds of flour, two pounds of beef and a pint of pease. Tears must have been shed over grace that evening. Within a day or two a pound of beef would be selling for three halfpence. Captain Browning lay dead upon the deck of his ship. He had been shot in the head as he had stood cheering on his men. He was killed on the spot. He died in sight of his native city, and his body was buried in the cathedral, next to Henry Baker's. King William eventually gave his widow a pension and tied a diamond chain about his neck with his own hands.

The British casualties were light, with only twelve killed and fewer wounded. The 28th July, as Ash noted in his diary, was a day to be greatly remembered. The citizens of Londonderry would remember it as long as they lived, for on that day they had been delivered from famine and slavery. They would have been threatened with famine if they were not able to hold out, and they would be slaves to James if they surrendered. The Lord had preserved the city from the enemy, and would always keep it in good hands.

The chaos along the walls had been loud when the city was relieved. Bonfires blazed all that night and the bells of Saint Columb's rang out, but the Catholic guns continued to roar in defiance. A random shot killed Alexander Lindesay and his daughter, who had been friends and neighbours of Walker's in his Tyrone parish. They had fled from Loughrey to take refuge in Londonderry.

When the Catholics heard that the city had been relieved, they decided to retreat, for the impregnable boom had been broken. On 31st July, said Ash, the enemy decamped and left the siege and burnt a great number of houses in County Londonderry. Walker wrote that on the last day of July they ran away in the night-time and robbed and burnt everywhere, leaving the country people with nothing. Next morning the Protestants went in pursuit of the fleeing Catholics, but seven Protestants were killed because they gave chase so easily. Kirke entered the city in triumph, marching his forces to Londonderry, and George Walker left for Scotland and England on a triumphant tour, eventually publishing his account of the siege. He was killed at the Battle of the Boyne in 1690. The siege of Londonderry lives on as one of the great sieges in British history. Starting with a severe disadvantage over the Catholics, the Protestants eventually held out; their cry had been "No Surrender!"

Select Bibliography

Brian Lacy, *Siege City* (The Blackstaff Press, 1990)

C D Milligan, *The Relief of Derry* (The Londonderry Sentinel, 1946)

Cecil Davis Milligan, *History of the Siege of Londonderry* (H R Carter Publication Ltd., 1889)

George Hill, *The Macdonnells of Antrim* (The Glens of Antrim Historical Society, 1976)

J G Simms, *Jacobite Ireland, 1685–91* (Routledge and Kegan Paul, 1969)

The Siege of Derry (APCK, 1966)

Oliver C Gibson, *The Western Protestant Army 1688/90* (Oliver C. Gibson, 1989)

Patrick Macrory, *The Siege of Derry* (Oxford University Press, 1988)

Peter Beresford Ellis, *The Boyne Water, The Battle of the Boyne 1690* (The Blackstaff Press, 1989)

Peter Robinson, *Their Cry Was "No Surrender"* (Crown Publications, 1988)

Philip Dwyer, *A True Account of the Siege of Londonderry. A Vindication of the Account of the Siege of Derry*

Sir Thomas Phillips, *Londonderry and the London Companies* (HMSO, 1928)

Thomas Witheroe, *Derry and Enniskillen in the Year 1689* (William Mullan, 1685–91)

T W Moody, *The Londonderry Plantation 1609–1641* (William Mullan & Sons, 1939)

Tony Gray, *No Surrender!* (Macdonald and Janes, 1975)

W A Maguire, *Kings in Conflict* (Blackstaff, 1990)